FAT
CHICKS
RULE!

FAT CHICKS RULE!

How to Survive in a Thin-Centric World

LARA FRATER

PUBLISHING

Book cover and interior design by Azadeh Houshyar.

Library of Congress Cataloging-in-Publication Data
Frater, Lara.
Fat chicks rule! : how to survive in a thin-centric world / Lara Frater.
p. cm.
Includes bibliographical references.
ISBN: 0-9752517-1-6
1. Overweight women—Health and hygiene—United States. 2. Overweight
women—United States—Social conditions. 3. Overweight women—Conduct of
life. 4. Overweight women—Psychology. 5. Discrimination against overweight
persons—United States. 6. Obesity in women—Social aspects—United States.
I. Title.

RC552.O25F73 2005
362.196'398'0082—dc22   2005009447

10-digit ISBN: 0-9752517-1-6
13-digit ISBN: 978-0-9752517-1-3

IG PUBLISHING
178 Clinton Avenue
Brooklyn, NY 11205
www.igpub.com

Printed in Canada
10 9 8 7 6 5 4 3 2 1

For Jon

*Fat bottomed girls,
you make the rocking world go round!*

QUEEN

Table of Contents

"I am what I am."

GOD

INTRODUCTION

I started to gain weight when I was ten. As I grew from a "pretty little girl" into a "chubby teenager," I noticed that people started treating me differently. From other kids came the expected insults — "Fatso," "Fattie," "Lard-Butt." At least I could yell back at them. But I couldn't say anything to "well-meaning" adults who would smile, touch my cheek, and with a concerned look, say, "You have such a pretty face, Lara — if you only lost some weight." So I internalized my feelings of confusion and shame.

By the time I was thirteen I weighed 160 pounds and no longer needed to be told by others that I was fat, as I had a new friend — my inner thin voice I liked to call it — who whispered lovely phrases to me like, "You are so fat, you are a whale, you are worthless unless you lose weight." I also looked the part of Moby Dick because I owned no cool clothes, since nothing cool came in my size.

I blamed my weight on everything I could think of: laziness, my psychological makeup (who hasn't heard the line, "It's not what she is eating, but what is eating her"), my parents, my roommates, magazines, drugs, Hollywood, sexism and capitalism. I felt that I couldn't accomplish anything in life as long as I was fat.

So I did what most other fat girls did — I began to diet. I'd confidently start one and follow it for a few weeks, certain that, after a few hard months of denial, I would wind up thin. I was positive that my soon-to-be thin body would give me all the things I felt I lacked: friends, success, beauty.

After a few weeks, however, feelings of deprivation would gnaw at me. Then, before you can say, "cheating on her diet," I would be bingeing on whole cakes, gallons of ice cream, big bowls of pasta, bread, you name it. Then, after a few weeks of pigging out, I would began yet another diet. As the TV commercial went when I was a kid, "And so on, and so on..."

By the time I was sixteen I weighed close to two hundred pounds. I decided it was time to put my money where my mouth was, and get serious about my weight problem. For the first (but not the last) time, I joined a pay for participation weight loss program. Every week, I would pay a fee to be weighed. (Thank God I didn't have to pay by the pound.) While I was standing on the scale, feeling like the fat lady at the circus, the group leader would talk about how happy and successful she was now that she was thin. She would come over to me, look at the scale, and excitedly tell the rest of the group, "Lara, you lost one pound this week!" Applause and congratulations would follow. The applause and congratulations would turn into "better luck next time" the following week when I had gained the pound back, or more.

For the next ten years or so, I went on — and off — every diet imaginable: shakes, portion control, diet foods, fad diets, over-the-counter drugs and supplements. (My favorite were AYDS — they tasted like caramels, and though the directions told you to eat three a day, I would often eat the whole box in an hour.) I tried everything to lose weight short of surgery, and if I'd had the money, I would be writing this book with my stomach stapled.

No matter what I tried, it all followed the same pattern: I'd lose a lot of weight very quickly, before hitting a plateau (usually after losing twenty to thirty pounds). To compensate for the decrease in my rate of weight loss, I would lower my food intake, or remove more foods from the eating plans I was on. But no matter what I did, I just couldn't lose any more weight. As my weight loss stopped, and my weight started to go back up, I would grow frustrated and miserable, until, having failed on yet another diet, I would explode with a massive binge.

On and on the cycle went. Diets, weight gain, weight loss, weight loss products. Until I finally got sick of it. Sick of worrying about everything that went into my mouth. Sick of obsessing about my weight. And most of all, sick of dieting!

Throwing the books and miracle cures in the trash, I swore off dieting forever. Then, with a bit of faith and a lot of fear, I started down an unknown road — the one called "eating normally."

I feared that uncontrollable binge eating and massive weight gain would follow. I feared that three hundred, four hundred, five hundred pounds of me would follow. However, to my surprise, as soon as I stopped dieting, my binge eating stopped. I came to realize that dieting had caused my bingeing because the act of eating had become black or white — either starvation on "healthy" foods or total bingeing. Without the pressure of having to worry about what I put into my mouth, I actually started eating better.

At the same time that I started eating normally, I discovered the fat acceptance movement. All of a sudden, after trying to fit my round body into the square hole of thin society, I found people who accepted their size as something that defined them in a positive light. Joining this movement made me realize that it wasn't the fat that was making me unhappy, it was me that was making me unhappy. And once I started to accept myself as a "fat chick," the image I had of myself started to change dramatically, even if the image in the mirror remained dramatic.

I still have my good and bad days. Some days I still look in the mirror and think I'm the fattest thing on earth, but other times — and they are starting to get more frequent — I love my body. And that is the most important thing: I am learning to love my fat self and to look at fat not as something abnormal that must be eliminated at all costs, but as the very essence of who I am!

Every day we are bombarded through the media, medical community and big business with what is considered the "ideal" image of the female form, what some call the "Barbie doll" look — no waist, no gut, no weight, 105 pounds soaking wet. Terry Poulton, author of *No Fat Chicks,* calls this "the billion-dollar brainwash," the linking of big business to the glorification of thinness.

In the non-ideal real world, however, 96 percent of women do not match up to the models and actresses presented in the media. The average model is 5'10" and weighs 110 pounds. The average woman is 5'4" and weighs 142 pounds. In addition, women are overwhelmed with statistics and images showing how fat is unhealthy and unattractive, as well as advertisements for diet books, programs and pills, and of course, the new phenomena of makeover television episodes that leave us with the message that it's *so* easy to lose weight. All this societal pressure gives many women a negative self-image about their bodies, since we are expected to fit into an impossible beauty ideal.

It is tempting to scream, "It's all the media's fault!" But, when it comes down to it, it is our bodies, so it is our responsibility. And, since we big people are clearly the majority in twenty-first-century America, we must take the discussion away from the thin minority who try to force their views on us. We must take our bodies back from the diet companies, television shows, and well-meaning and not-so-well-meaning people who tell us that fat is bad, unattractive, unhealthy, abnormal.

My little contribution to the battle for the bulge is this book. I want to help end the cycle of destruction that dieting and lack of self-esteem leads to, and help my fellow fat chicks accept two important things:

You are beautiful even if you don't measure up to the Hollywood standard of beauty.

There is no perfect number, perfect weight, perfect size or perfect body, except what you think is perfect for you.

I want to help you accept your size and keep your mind, body and spirit fit without pushing yourself into unrealistic ideals and fantasies. Fat acceptance is about not fantasizing; it's about saying, "This is what I weigh, and I need to get on the business of living right now, not fifty pounds from now."

But I don't want you to just be a fat woman who accepts yourself — I want you to be a FAT CHICK WHO RULES! And that means not only accepting yourself, but doing something with that acceptance. That is why I wrote this book — not only to help you feel good inside, but also to help you deal with many of the practical, day-to-day issues that fat chicks face in today's thin-centric world — issues such as shopping, beauty, sex, entertainment, discrimination, the straight talk on obesity and dieting, and much, much more. I want this book to be the ultimate guide to all obstacles, both spiritual and practical, that fat chicks face today!

So, as the battle for our bodies wages on against the tummy tucks, stomach staples, miracle diets and fat-hating medical community, I hope that this book can be just one small (but not too small) piece of the war against our fat-phobic culture. And to all of my fat sisters (and brothers, too), let me tell you that a true fat movement is sweeping the nation — a movement toward fat acceptance.

"In many cultures and historical periods women have been proud to be large — being fat was a sign of fertility, of prosperity, of the ability to survive."

OUR BODIES, OURSELVES

CHAPTER ONE

THE FAT-ASTIC
HISTORY OF FAT CHICKS

The most famous early image of a woman is the Venus de Willendorf, created out of limestone approximately 26,000 years ago. And you know what? She's a fat chick, with large breasts, an even larger belly, and thighs large enough to crush ten Calvin Klein models at once. Back then, fat on a woman was a sign of well-being and plenty, and also indicated the ability to survive hard times. In the days when hunting provided a large proportion of food, having a fat wife was the equivalent of driving a Porsche. Since her discovery in 1908, the Venus has become the premier image of prehistoric art and the female form.

Another important early form is the *Goddess of Laussel*, a limestone carving found in France, which is estimated to be about 25,000 years old. She is a large woman, apparently pregnant, with big breasts and hips.

The celebration of fat women continued through the Renaissance, when many artists painted fleshy women with wide hips and muscular arms (size 16's at least!). One of the most famous was Peter Paul Rubens (1577–1640), who painted Venus, Diana and Andromeda. Other artists whose vision of beauty was the large woman were Titian (Tiziano Vecellio, 1485–1576), Rembrandt and Da Vinci. While female images had become smaller by the end of the Renaissance, artists such as Francois Boucher were still painting lovely, fleshy women.

The nineteenth century marked the beginning of the battle against fat. On one hand, plumpness was still fashionable in the Victorian era, as physicians believed that fat cells were crucial to a well-balanced personality. On the other hand, health reformers such as the Reverend Sylvester Graham, creator of the graham cracker, believed that immortality was because of the sin of gluttony, and started to rail against what they saw as America's sinful overeating habits.

There was also the evolution of dieting as a concept. As Peter Stearns points out in his book *Fat History: Bodies and Beauties in the Modern West*, during the nineteenth century, "the word 'diet' began its evolution from its initial meaning in English, of a regimen specifying certain types of food to remedy illness, to its modern usage of losing weight." Other nineteenth-century issues that lead the Western world toward a thin ideal included notions of slender beauty postulated by Romantic poets and changes in fashion toward more formfitting clothing.

In the 1890s, chemist Wilbur Atwater conceived of measuring the heat value of food groups by burning the nutritional components and determining the amount of heat they gave off. Thus, the calorie was born.

By the dawn of the twentieth century, attitudes toward weight began to radically shift. Obesity, which had not been considered harmful, became a "disease," based on the lack of thyroid hormone. This reclassification was accompanied by the first advertisements for products to promote weight loss, many of which contained dangerous chemicals such as arsenic, digitalis and strychnine.

In 1919, Dr. Lulu Hunt Peters published the book *Diet and Health With a Key to the Calories*, the first book to advocate a specific daily caloric intake (1,200 per day!). Peters believed that successful dieting demanded lifelong vigilance, hardship and suffering. In addition, she stated that calorie control equaled weight control, and therefore, people who were unable to manage their weight simply had no self-control (the "fat people lack self-control" argument). *Diet and Health With a Key to the Calories* sold two million copies.

At the same time, the flapper look became a popular style for women. While its tall, thin look symbolized fashion freedom for women because they no longer had to wear corsets, it also caged them into having to look slim. Women were also able for the first time to express an appetite for sex, which was combined with the notion championed by Peters and others that fat was due to weakness of character. "Dieting was a way, again, to express virtue and self-control even in a changing sexual climate," Peter Stearns writes.

Despite the popularity of the new flapper look, the Miss Americas of the early twentieth century still had BMIs (Body Mass Indexes) of between 20 and 25. (Today, Miss America has a BMI of 18.5, which is considered medically underweight.) In addition, the typical flapper was 5'7" and 140 pounds, which is considered a normal BMI today. Symbols of new freedom they may have been, flappers weren't super thin.

The trend toward dieting and thinness continued through the Great Depression. According to Hillel Schwartz in *Never Satisfied: A Cultural History of Diets, Fantasies and Fat*, by 1936, over 100,000 people were taking dinitrophenol, a chemical derived from benzene and used in industrial dyes, to treat obesity. Many suffered horrible side effects from this drug, including rashes, blindness and death. Amphetamines and digitalis were also used to put the fat chick in her thin place.

While buxom beauties such as Marilyn Monroe were all the rage in the 1950s, the rise of media and television continued the trend toward the thin. In addition, women's magazines started to jump on the diet bandwagon, with ridiculous articles like "Lose Weight While You're Pregnant." Reading materials in the 1950s also played up the dichotomy between the sexes, as boys were encouraged to eat more to build up their muscles, strength and endurance (drink your milk!), while girls needed to learn self-control when eating. Also, in 1963, Weight Watchers was founded as a support group for women who wanted to lose weight.

Although the late 1960s were a time of liberation for many women, they weren't for fat chicks. This is best represented by the emergence in 1967 of the 5'7'', 97-pound model Twiggy, who made the malnourished look all the rage. By the early 1970s, 49 percent of women were on diets (compared with 14 percent in 1950). The dieting industry's primary target had been captured.

However, hope was on the way! The National Association to Advance Fat Acceptance (NAAFA) started in 1969, first as a social group, then growing and expanding to become more politically active. The Fat Underground grew out of NAAFA because of a desire for a more radical approach to fight size discrimination. Using guerrilla tactics, they often "raided" weight loss classes to spread a message of fat acceptance and social change. They also joined feminist marches and sent in papers to progressive publishers, academic health organizations and the media.

But as few others championed "fat acceptance," attitudes against the pleasingly plump continued to grow. By 1987, the average female model — the ideal — weighed 23 percent less than the average American woman. The 1980s and '90s also featured the rise of eating disorders such as bulimia and anorexia, the dieting obsession, weight loss surgery, and the cultural ascension of underweight look in the fashion world, known as "heroin chic," the natural outgrowth of the Twiggy phenomena.

In 2004, the battle continues, with the dieting industry, the media and much of the medical establishment on the "thin is good, fat is death" side, and activists like Marilyn Wann, Jennifer Weiner, Paul Campos, Laura Fraser and yours truly on the "accept your body, embrace your weight" side. Hopefully, we can tip the scales (pun intended) to our side, and start to write a brand-new, size-positive history of fat chicks!

"If vous mean a heavenly body the world lusts after, yes. If vous mean the other way, vous can't run fast enough."

MISS PIGGY IN A TV GUIDE INTERVIEW IN WHICH SHE WAS ASKED
IF HOLLYWOOD TREATS HER LIKE A PIECE OF MEAT
BECAUSE OF HER CURVY FIGURE.

CHAPTER 2

ROLL MODELS:
Famous Fat Chicks

The Legends

ELIZABETH CADY STANTON (1815–1902)

The nineteenth-century feminist, catalyst of the women's rights movement, was praised for her robust figure. Today, she would have had a BMI of 40.

LILLIAN "DIAMOND LIL" RUSSELL (1861–1922)

Weighing over 230 pounds, she was the pioneer for the large, buxom actress, and an inspiration for, among others, Mae West and Marilyn Monroe. She appeared in countless operas and musicals. At the height of her fame, girls wore padding to mimic her voluptuous shape.

KATIE SANDWINA (1884–1952)

Six-foot-one and 209 pounds, Katie twisted steel bars in a vaudeville act as a teenager, later becoming a star for the Barnum & Bailey Circus. Posters referred to her as "Germany's Herculean Venus, the Most Perfect Female Figure, the Strongest Woman that Ever Lived."

SOPHIE TUCKER (1884–1966)

Playing piano to accompany her sister at amateur shows, Sophie was called "the fat girl." At first she was required to wear blackface since she was "so big and ugly." One night she went on without her blackface and was a hit. Tucker used songs like "I Don't Want to Be Thin" and "Nobody Loves a Fat Girl, But Oh How a Fat Girl Can Love" to emphasize her "fat girl" image with humor and sexuality.

MAE WEST (1893–1980)

"I never worry about diets. The only carrots that interest me are the number you get in a diamond."

KATE SMITH (1907–1986)

Although her grandparents and parents had great musical talent, they disapproved of the life of the professional entertainer, as they feared that Kate, a beautiful plus-size young woman weighing around 300 pounds, would be ridiculed about her weight if she were to enter showbiz. But her desire to sing led her to quit school and move to New York in 1926. Originally she was wanted for comedic "fat girl" roles. Her chance as a full-time singer came in 1930 when Ted Collins, an executive with Columbia Records, developed the radio show "Kate Smith Sings" (CBS,

1931–47), which became one of the most popular programs of the 1930s and early '40s. The song that she is most closely associated with is Irving Berlin's "God Bless America," which she introduced on Armistice Day, 1938, and for which the composer granted her exclusive rights to sing on the air.

....

MAHALIA JACKSON (1911–1972)
Absorbing the sounds of blues singers like Ma Rainey and Bessie Smith, the Queen of Gospel Music's charismatic performing style influenced many, including Aretha Franklin. Her "singing weight" was 200 pounds, but sometimes, she said, "my good Louisiana cooking makes it shoot up to something like 240."

....

ELLA FITZGERALD (1917–1996)
Orphaned at the age of 15, Ella lived for a time on the streets of Harlem, earning her living by singing and dancing for a few dollars. When she began regularly singing with the Chick Webb band, audiences didn't care about her size, simply falling in love with her untrained voice that was able to span three octaves with ease.

....

BIG MAMA THORNTON (1926–1984)
Her real name was Willie Mae, but after her first show at the Apollo in 1952, she was nicknamed "Big Mama" and it stuck. Six feet tall and 300 pounds, she could sing with a power to surpass many noted male singers. More than any other figure in the history of rhythm and blues, she typified the rough, brassy female blues shouter after which Janice Joplin styled herself. Her best-known record is "Hound Dog," which

Elvis Presley chose, after hearing her recorded version of the song, for his second attempt at a hit.

TOTIE FIELDS (1930–1978)

An ancestor to the proudly unapologetic style of Roseanne Barr, Totie Fields was one of the few female comics of her day to utilize the bold "sizzle and sputter" style of male comics like Alan King and Buddy Hackett. A New York-accented yenta who performed self-deflating fat jokes amid her extroverted kvetching shtick, Totie began performing in the Catskills in the early 1960s, when women weren't necessarily expected to offer their opinions or ideas. Totie did, though, treating the crowd like friends and inflating stories about everyday events to comic proportions.

SHELLEY WINTERS (1922–)

Actress. "I'm not overweight. I'm just nine inches too short."

ARETHA FRANKLIN (1942–)

"I can be pleasingly plump if need be until I can work it off. Or as my friend says, 'I can be a plump cutie.' I can be a plump cutie until I can work it off. Everybody doesn't like thin girls. I'm with Mo'Nique. Mo'Nique knows what she's talking about."

NELL CARTER (1948–2003)

Carter was nominated for two Emmys for her role as housekeeper Nell Harper on the show "Gimme A Break!" Outspoken about her weight, she had been yo-yo dieting for years upon her death in 2003 from heart disease complicated by diabetes.

"MAMA" CASS ELLIOT (1941–1974)

The most beloved member of the Mamas & the Papas because of her incredible voice, Cass went on to record six solo albums and had numerous charting singles after the group split up in 1966. She also headlined in Las Vegas, starred in several television specials and guest hosted the "Tonight Show" no less than a dozen times. While on tour in the United Kingdom in July 1974, she died of a massive heart attack, after years of crash dieting had weakened her heart to the point of failure. An urban legend of her death that has her choking on a sandwich is false and only furthers fat stereotypes.

Today's Heroes

KATHY BATES

Commenting on losing the lead role in the movie version of "Frankie and Johnny" to Michelle Pfeiffer (even though she had won an Obie and an L.A. Drama Critics Award for playing the role on Broadway), Kathy said, "It was hard, not just for the lack of work but because you have to face up to how people are looking at you. And you think, 'Well, y'know, I'm a real person.' "

DELTA BURKE

A former beauty queen, Delta has spent a lifetime fighting her weight. She turned to speed to help her lose weight during her time on *Designing Women* and was eventually fired from the show because of her size. Unlike Oprah, Delta has finally accepted herself and her size. She now designs clothes for larger women under the label Delta Burke Designs. She is also the author of *Delta Style: Eve Wasn't a Size 6 and Neither Am I*, which is part autobiography and part style guide for larger women.

MARGARET CHO

Cho is a sexy and chubby comedian who has struggled at times because she is not conventionally attractive or willing to play the submissive Asian. In her comedy film *I'm the One that I Want* she rants about how TV producers insisted she diet for her TV show *All American Girl*. She followed their instructions, lost 30 pounds in two weeks and put herself in the hospital with kidney failure. In *Notorious CHO*, she tells how she refuses to subscribe to any more diets and is happy the way she is. She also has her own clothing line for sizes 10 to 18.

MINDY COHN

Cohn made the role of chubby, wisecracking Natalie Green on the 1980s TV show *Facts of Life* into something especially size-positive. Natalie has a healthy self-image as an active member of the school newspaper staff, which she hopes will prepare her for a future as a writer. "I'd rather be a happy Magic Marker than a skinny pencil," says Natalie — and she means it.

KIM COLES

The beautiful star of *Living Single* (along with Queen Latifah), Kim has also been a model for plus-size store Lane Bryant. (She is a proud size 16.) In 1990 she was fired from *In Living Color* for refusing to participate in sketches that made fun of her being fat. She wrote a hilarious book on single life called *I'm Free but It Will Cost You*, in which she talks about her dieting battles. "After five months, I was a svelte size 8. I was hot, right? I got work, right? Yes, yes. I was happy, right? Wrong. I was hungry and tired. And I missed cheesecake."

....

LYNNE COX

Perhaps the best cold-water swimmer ever. With a body density precisely that of seawater, her 36-percent body fat gives her neutral buoyancy. Her most famous swim was in 1987 when she completed 2.7 miles in the Bering Straits, 350 miles north of Anchorage, Alaska, where the water temperature ranges from 38 to 42 degrees Fahrenheit. Brrr!

....

EMME

According to her autobiography, True Beauty, Emme dieted and binged for years. She has a clothing line for sizes 12 to 24 and has written Life's Little Emergencies, a book on fashion and beauty tips. She even has her own doll. She was twice voted by People magazine as one of the most beautiful people in the world. She starred in the movie Curve, a documentary on plus-size models.

....

CONCHATA FERRELL

Long before Camryn Manheim shouted, "This is for all the fat girls!" Conchata Ferrell was toiling away unnoticed in the background of many a movie and TV series as the designated Hollywood "fat girl." Among her numerous credits is an Obie Award for her performance in *The Sea Horse* in 1973, and roles in movies such as *Network, Mystic Pizza* and *Edward Scissorhands*, to name but a few. She was also a regular on "L.A. Law."

DAWN FRENCH

A plus-size actress who has lectured against fat discrimination, Dawn is half of the comedy team of French and Saunders, as well as one of the most successful comediennes in England. She refuses to diet and has created a video called "Dawn French on Big Women," in which she deals with issues affecting fat women. "If I had been around when Rubens was painting, I would have been revered as a fabulous model. Kate Moss? Well, she would have been the paintbrush."

DEE HAKALA

At 220 pounds, Dee Hakala's message is that you don't need a "hard body" to be healthy. Dee launched a revolutionary fitness program called "The New Face of Fitness" for the thousands of Americans who feel left behind by the diet and fitness industry. Her program was chosen as the winner of the Nike Corporation's inaugural Fitness Innovation Award, providing her with a grant to launch her fitness plan, which is now operating in YWCAs and other facilities across the country.

CHERYL HAWORTH

At 5'9'' and 307 pounds, Cheryl can bench-press almost 500 pounds and is a three-time national champion holding every record in her weight class. She took the bronze medal in the 2000 Olympics in Sydney, Australia. I would like to see anyone make fun of her weight to her face.

CANDYE KANE

Born in East Los Angeles, Candye always dreamed of being a singer. Early on, to support herself and her young son, she became a nude model, appearing on the covers of *Hustler*, *Juggs* and *Floppers*. Simultaneously, she became involved in the burgeoning punk rock music scene of the early 1980s. In 1986, she was signed by CBS Records, but the label dropped her when she refused to lose weight and renounce her past. Eventually, she found a home in the blues and has recorded six best-selling CDs to date, plays 250 shows a year all over the world and has appeared on countless television shows.

QUEEN LATIFAH

Actress and singer. "To me, though, all women are beautiful. Every woman is a queen and we all have different things to offer."

CAMRYN MANHEIM

In 1998, during her acceptance speech for winning the Emmy for Best Supporting Actress in a drama series for her role of Eleanor Frutt on "The Practice," she screamed out, "This is for all the fat girls!" In her engaging memoir, *Wake Up, I'm Fat*, she writes about her plight as a fat actress making her way in a thin world.

MO'NIQUE

Actress. "I'm comfortable with fat, chubby, plump, porky, big girl — whatever you think you wanna say, I'm comfortable with that."

KATHY NAJIMY

A comedic actress and the queen of supporting roles. On her Web site she says, "Women are vital and beautiful at all weights and sizes. There is NO one way we are supposed to be, although the world will tell us every day that we only have one option. That is not true."

ROSIE O'DONNELL

Despite sometimes being pro-diet, Rosie is proof that a plus-size actress can succeed today. Rosie has done it all: stand-up comic, drama, writer and talk show host.

MISS PIGGY

If anyone gets in her way, she cuts them down with a karate chop. Aggressively pursued Kermit until he married her. *Hi Yah!*

JENNIFER PORTNICK

A 240-pound fitness instructor who was told she was too fat to teach at Jazzercise, she filed a discrimination complaint against the company under the San Francisco anti-fat discrimination law. Today, Jazzercise hires its instructors based on fitness, not size.

ROSEANNE

A trailblazer for all fat chicks, Roseanne Barr broke the fat woman taboo when she began talking about her weight in her stand-up routines in the 1980s. At its peak, Roseanne was the highest rated show on television. Sadly, like many female celebrities, she eventually gave way to the pressure to be thin and began a round of dieting and plastic surgery. She hosted the Lane Bryant Fashion Show in 2003 and now seems to be back on the size-acceptance bandwagon.

MARILYN WANN

My favorite 270-pound activist is the author of the best-selling book on fat acceptance, *FAT! SO?* She also performs with the Bod Squad, a group of plus-size cheerleaders who promote the idea that fat is beautiful. She was instrumental in getting San Francisco to pass a landmark anti-discrimination law to protect fat people. In an interview with *Stanford Magazine* in 2003, she said, "The closet for a fat person is an unlived life, full of self hatred... Fat people are the last acceptable targets of discrimination."

WENDY WASSERSTEIN

Author. "A diet counselor once told me that all overweight people are angry with their mothers and channel their frustrations into overeating. So I guess that means all thin people are happy, calm and have resolved their Oedipal entanglements."

MARISSA JARET WINOKUR

Known for her memorable roles in *American Beauty* and *Scary Movie*, Marissa Jaret Winokur won the 2003 Tony for Leading Actress in a Musical for playing Tracy Turnblad in the Broadway musical *Hairspray*. When she accepted her Tony award, she said, "If a 4-foot-11, chubby New York girl can be a leading lady in a Broadway show and win a Tony, then anything can happen!"

"I'm sure many of the other home viewers out there are pleasantly plump or chunky."

TRACY TURNBLAD, HAIRSPRAY

CHAPTER 3

HERE WE ARE NOW, ENTERTAIN US!

Entertainment for Fat Chicks

A study conducted by Michigan State University examined portrayals of overweight characters in 275 episodes from 56 different series for the 1999–2000 television season. According to Professor Bradley Greenberg, who headed the study, "The female differences were staggering. Whereas one in four American women in reality is obese, the TV figure is three in 100. And whereas 5 percent of all women in reality are underweight, nearly one in three on television has that body type." Greenberg added that half of all women in real life are average or underweight, yet on TV the number is almost nine out of every ten. He concluded that "the extent to which the overweight individual is absent or minimized on television provides new evidence that warrants our attention. Generally, if the mass media omit or ignore a particular group, such groups are deemed of lesser value and importance." Television reflects a society not like our own, where the majority are thin. This, of course, puts immense psychological pressure on women to conform to the ideal standard that television and movies dictate. Shouldn't we all be like the Monica character from *Friends*, who used to be fat, but miraculously managed to join the 3 to 5 percent of people who diet and keep all the weight off?

Even when fat chicks are portrayed in television or film, they are usually seen as binge eaters, negative or evil characters, sidekicks, or thin actors in fat suits (good ol' Monica again!).

But all is not lost. There are TV shows and movies that have large women as their center of attention, or as significant supporting characters. The following is a list of movies and TV shows that feature fat women in a positive light.

Section 1: **Movies**

ABOUT SCHMIDT
Kathy Bates nude in a hot tub. 'Nuff said.

BABY CAKES
Ricki Lake stars as Grace, a fat and lonely mortician, who falls in love with Rob, a hunky subway conductor, who happens to have a girlfriend. When Grace learns that Rob's girlfriend is out of town, she decides to woo him. At first Rob isn't interested in her romantically, but as he gets to know her, he discovers that he enjoys Grace's company, and in the end, the fat chick gets the guy — without losing a pound. This is a remake of a German film called *Zuckerbaby*, which I also recommend.

BAGDAD CAFÉ

German actress Marianne Sagebrecht stars as Jasmin, a German tourist who dumps her husband in the middle of the desert, then finds herself at the Bagdad Café, a run-down truck stop and motel owned by the unhappy Brenda. At first, Brenda is suspicious of Jasmin, but a friendship eventually grows between the two women, which changes both them and the town for the better. Plus-size Sagebrecht shines as the movie's sex symbol.

BEAUTIFUL GIRL

The typical feel-good family movie, with one exception — the main character is large-sized Becca Wassermann, played by Marissa Jaret Winokur. Becca is a music teacher who gets caught up in trying to be beautiful when she decides to compete against a high school rival in a beauty pageant. Eventually, Becca realizes that being herself is more important than winning.

BRIDGET JONES' DIARY

The slightly chubby Bridget Jones, played by Renée Zellweger, becomes determined to change her life with a New Years Resolution and a diary. The good point about this movie is that she meets a man who loves her chubby body. The bad point is that the naturally thin Renee Zellweger gained 25 pounds for the role.

CIRCLE OF FRIENDS

Minnie Driver, who gained 30 pounds for the movie, plays Benny Hogan, a smart, shy woman who attends the University of Dublin in 1950s Ireland. Benny's self-esteem is regularly worn down by her beautiful friend Nan and a creepy suitor named Sean who both tell her she's unattractive and fat. In the end, though, Benny overcomes her self-esteem issues and becomes a strong and confident woman — and gets the man, instead of the "prettier" Nan. This movie has a great size-positive message (even if a thin actress was cast in the lead).

CURVE

A funny and upbeat documentary about plus-size models and the fashion industry featuring Emme and Kathy Najimy, *Curve* examines the fashion world's prejudice against larger women, and the huge disconnect between statistics and reality.

FRIED GREEN TOMATOES

Kathy Bates stars as Evelyn Couch, a neglected housewife who gains self-confidence after meeting Ninny and hearing her stories about growing up. Unfortunately, one of Evelyn's problems is that she thinks she eats too much, so her new self-esteem comes partly with carrot sticks.

THE GIRL MOST LIKELY TO...

This black comedy stars Stockard Channing as a homely and overweight woman who, following plastic surgery after a car accident, becomes thin and beautiful, and decides to kill all those who wronged her. You'll cheer each time she wipes out another one of the fatphobic!

HAIRSPRAY

John Waters' 1980s film *Hairspray* takes the cake as the best fat-positive movie ever. Set in early 1960s Baltimore, the once-fat-chick Ricki Lake stars as Tracy Turnblad, who is "pleasantly plump" and dreams of appearing on the Corny Collins Dance Show. Not only does she get on the show, but she becomes more popular than the thin and blonde Amber, and gets the hunky guy in the end. This movie has a huge cult following and was made into a successful Broadway musical in 2002.

MORE TO LOVE

Plus-size Maryanne, played by Louise Werner, lives an isolated life as a secretary at an adult supply store, where she is ridiculed by her thin coworkers. Her life changes when she meets Fran, who helps her become a woman with confidence. Best of all, as Maryanne's life improves dramatically, her coworkers' lives fall apart.

MURIEL'S WEDDING

Toni Collette plays Muriel, a fat and slightly dim young woman whose dream is to escape small-town Australia and get married. The only problem is that she has no money (or boyfriend). When things don't go the way she plans, Muriel steals money from her family and runs off with her friend Rhonda to the city, where she discovers that it isn't marriage she wants, but a little self-esteem. Collette gained forty pounds for the role of Muriel. I guess there were no actual fat actresses available?

REAL WOMEN HAVE CURVES

This movie is one of the few dramas to have a real plus-size woman in a lead role. It is the story of Ana, a chubby Mexican-American teenager who lives with her family in East Los Angeles. Upon her graduation from high school, Ana is awarded a scholarship to Columbia University, which conflicts with the beliefs of her traditional, old-world parents, who want Ana to work to help support the family instead. Her mother would also like Ana to lose some weight. Torn between her dreams for college and her cultural heritage she agrees to work with her mother at her sister's sewing factory, and learns to admire the female factory workers, who teach her solidarity and teamwork. At the end, Ana leaves for college, realizing that leaving home to continue her education is essential to finding her place in the world.

ROSALIE GOES SHOPPING

Plus-size German actress Marianne Sagebrecht starred as Rosalie, a smart, sexy, loving wife and mother who, in order to support her family financially, becomes deeply involved in embezzling. I love this movie because it features a full-figured woman as a sex symbol with a husband who adores her.

SECRET SOCIETY

Charlotte Brittain stars as Daisy, a young fat chick with a doting husband who is also ashamed of her body. When her husband loses his job, she is forced to take a job at a factory, where she notices that plus-size manager Marlene gives special privileges to the other plus-size female coworkers. Eventually, Daisy finds out that the large women of the factory are members of a secret sumo wrestling society. Daisy joins them, and through sumo, gains confidence and becomes more assertive in her life.

ALSO WORTH A LOOK:

CLAIRE MAKES IT BIG

This is a hard to find short that stars Mara Hobel as plus-size actress Claire, who is tired of being passed over for roles in favor of thinner but less talented girls. She "enhances" a movie by substituting herself in place of another actress, receives rave reviews and is celebrated across the country. Loosely based on Kathy Bates losing her role in *Frankie and Johnny* after successfully playing it on Broadway.

GORGEOUS

Animated short by Kaz Cooke about Hermoine, a young and hip Australian who thinks she is fat. Hermoine's confidence is further ruined by the insecurity fairy Dierdre who gets her to starve, purge, torture herself with exercise and buy tons of makeup. After talking to large women, Hermoine finally has the confidence to drive Dierdre away.

DAWN FRENCH ON BIG WOMEN

The successful British comedian talks about big and beautiful fat women in photography, media and fashion.

Section 2: **Television**

....

AMERICAN IDOL

Although some of the participants in this weekly talent show are belittled for their weight, it still features large-sized talent that proves as good as its thin counterparts, if not even better. One of the plus-size contestants, Frenchie Davis, was awarded a role on Broadway in Rent, recorded a CD and played the lead in *Dreamgirls*.

....

BABES

A short-lived television show on Fox concerning the lives of three large-size sisters as they deal with life and being fat. Although it was marvelous to see a show about fat chicks, fat jokes were an integral part of the show's humor.

....

DELTA

Delta Burke stars as Delta Bishop, an aspiring country singer who happens to be plus-sized. Unfortunately, it lasted only a season.

....

THE FACTS OF LIFE

For us fat chicks who grew up in the eighties, Natalie (Mindy Cohn) was the teenager we all hoped to be. Smart, funny, fat and focused, she was also the first girl on the show (which was about four girls who meet in a boarding school) to lose her virginity.

FRENCH AND SAUNDERS

Dawn French and her partner, Jennifer Saunders, star in this British sketch comedy show. Dawn plays a variety of roles — sarcastic schoolgirl, sexy pop star, Pamela Anderson, Madonna, even an old man — and shows that plus-size women can do all types of comedy, not just physical fat jokes.

LESS THAN PERFECT

Sara Rue plays Claude, a chunky employee of a news network who becomes the personal assistant to the bigwig anchor, which invites resentment from her new colleagues. Fat chick Sherri Shepherd costars as Claude's friend Ramona. Kudos to this show for having two chubby ladies in the cast!

LIVING SINGLE

Living Single revolved around four single African American women who share a house together. The show starred the beautiful and big Queen Latifah as assertive Khadijah and size-sixteen Kim Coles as her sweet sister Synclair. This highly successful show ran for five seasons. This is one of the few successful sitcoms lead by plus-size actresses that featured positive role models.

ONE LIFE TO LIVE

Wowee! A soap opera that features a hip, big woman, with the plus-size Kathy Brier playing Marcie Walsh. Marcie started as a recurring character in 2002, and became so popular that she was made a regular. She even got a hunky boyfriend who died, but fans were so outraged over the breakup of this super couple that the producers brought him back from the dead.

THE PARKERS

With three lovely, large women in the cast, this show is a rarity on television. It stars large-size comedienne Mo'Nique as Nikki Parker, chubby Countess Vaughn as her daughter (Kim), and the plus-size Yvette Wilson as Nikki's friend Andell. According to Black Entertainment Television, The Parkers is the second highest rated show among black households.

THE PRACTICE

Set in Boston, *The Practice* centers on a firm of very passionate lawyers. Camryn Manhiem stars in a groundbreaking role as the eccentric and boisterous partner, Eleanor Frutt. This is the only drama on television in which the fat chick has a position of power.

ROSEANNE

Revolving around plus-size — at the time — Roseanne Barr, this sitcom was a groundbreaking (and highly successful) portrait of a lower-middle-class family in which both parents were fat. In one famous episode, Roseanne's husband Dan (John Goodman) fantasizes about another woman, whom Roseanne discovers also happens to be plus-size. *Roseanne* proved that a fat chick could star in a highly successful sitcom.

THE ROSEANNE BARR SHOW

Before Roseanne's big sitcom, she had a short-lived comedy show of her stand-up routines. Many of her original rants about weight, men and housework can be seen here.

THE STEVE HARVEY SHOW

This is one of the rare shows with a plus-size teen, Lori Beth Denberg.

TWO FAT LADIES

In this short-lived British cooking show, plus-size Clarissa Dickson-Wright and the late Jennifer Paterson traveled in a motorcycle and sidecar to scenic locations to cook up delicious food.

VERONICA'S CLOSET

Kathy Najimy stars as Veronica's right-hand woman. It's nice to see a plus-size character on a show about fashion.

WOMEN OF THE HOUSE

A spin-off of *Designing Women*. This time around, Delta Burke got to be whatever size she wanted. Unfortunately, the show was canceled after one season.

Section 3: **Fat Chick Lit**

For those who enjoy a good book, here is some great fat-positive literature, running the gamut from trashy romances to activist nonfiction. They may not all be masterpieces, but they do have one thing in common — they feature fat chicks that rule!

Mysteries

JOSEPHINE FULLER MYSTERIES by Lynne Murray

Lynne Murray's mysteries feature Josephine "Jo" Fuller, an amateur sleuth who is plus-sized and has plenty of attitude. Working as an investigator for San Diego philanthropist Alicia Madrone, she evaluates potential charities to see if they are worthy of Ms. Madrone's money. Each story involves a number of positive large-size characters and chubby chasers.

ODELIA GREY MYSTERIES by Sue Ann Jaffarian

This features large-size amateur detective Odelia Grey, a middle-aged single paralegal who is bored with her job until she is thrown into the secret world of her plus-size friend Sophie London, who has commited suicide. Or, was she a victim of murder?

NO. 1 LADIES' DETECTIVE AGENCY by Alexander McCall Smith

Precious Ramotswe is an unusual detective, in that she is female, fat and lives in Botswana. She is loved for her size because some people in Botswana believe that being fat is preferable. The other books in the series are *Tears of the Giraffe*, *Morality for the Beautiful Girls*, *The Kalahari Typing School for Men* and *The Full Cupboard of Life*.

Horror/Sci-fi/Fantasy

SUCH A PRETTY FACE, Edited by Lee Martindale

Several of the stories in this anthology focus on fat women, such as "Worse than the Curse" by Elizabeth Ann Scarborough, in which a princess gets the prince by being plump rather than thin; "Demon Bone" by Teresa Noelle Roberts, in which a young princess is possessed by a demon dying of anorexia; and "Polyformus Perfectus" by Paula L. Fleming, wherein a plus-size fitness instructor and three fat aliens must battle hostile aliens who have boarded their ship. My personal favorite is "Nuclear Winter" by Selina Rosen, in which only fat people survive an atomic war.

Fiction

ALL OF ME: A VOLUPTUOUS TALE by Venise Berry

Heroine Serpentine Williamson is a television reporter and a full-figured African American woman who attempts to commit suicide because of her damaged self-image and constant struggle to lose weight. Through therapy, a journal and reminiscences of her past, Serpentine gains self-esteem and, most importantly, size acceptance.

GOOD IN BED by Jennifer Weiner

Candace "Cannie" Shapiro finds out that her ex-boyfriend is writing a magazine column about their relationship, in which he reveals how size 16 Cannie broke it off with him because she couldn't accept his love. At first she is angry, but later she realizes that there are more important things to worry about than her size, which she learns to accept.

THE WAY IT IS by Patrick Sanchez

Three women — Ruby Waters, who loathes her fat body, Wanda, a large-size African-American model who is not embarrassed by her eating habits, and Simone, a thin news anchorwoman who is secretly binging and purging — share a house and learn about the joys of fat acceptance and the horrors of bulimia.

QUICK PICKS

• IN HER SHOES by Jennifer Weiner

• THE FOLLY OF ASSUMPTION, Edited by Lee Martindale

Romance

THE INDEPENDENT BRIDE by Sophie Weston

After being disinherited by her grandmother, who calls her a "potato," size 14 Pepper Calhoun runs off to London to start a business selling fabulous clothes for plus-size women.

WANTED: ONE GROOM by Pat Ballard

Large and beautiful Hanna Rockwell must marry by age thirty or lose her inheritance. However, when Matt Corbett, a singer down on his luck, agrees to marry Hanna "sight-unseen," she doesn't believe that he can love a fat chick like her.

SAY YOU'RE MINE by Judi McCoy

Full-figured Libby gets involved with a charming man who claims he is a ship captain from 200 years ago.

A WORTHY HEIR by Pat Ballard

Full-figured Pamela Spencer wants hospital care for her wheelchair-bound brother and accepts a job as a "replacement heir." When the real heir, a hunky man, shows up, sparks fly.

NOBODY'S PERFECT by Pat Ballard

Nella marries a man she doesn't love so he can have a mother for his child and she can keep her family's house. Her husband wonders if he can love a plus-size woman.

SUDDENLY YOU by Lisa Kleypas

It's early nineteenth-century London and virginal, full-figured novelist Amanda Briers decides to hire a male prostitute to "deflower" her. Instead, she meets publisher Jack Devlin and they instantly fall in love.

QUICK PICKS

- THE HIGH PRICE OF A GOOD MAN by Debra Phillips

- THE LOOK OF LOVE by Monica Jackson

- LIVING LARGE (ANTHOLOGY)

- A WHOLE LOTTA LOVE (ANTHOLOGY)

Young Adult

THE EARTH, MY BUTT AND OTHER ROUND THINGS by Carolyn Mackler

Fifteen-year-old fat teenager Virginia "Gin" Shreves thinks she was switched at birth because she is fat and her family is thin.

THE FAT CAMP COMMANDOS by Daniel Pinkwater

Follow the adventures of Sylvia and Ralph Nebula (and their friend Celtic Witch Mavis Goldfarg), who escape from fat camp after their parents trick them into attending.

FAT CHANCE by Leslea Newman

A sad but upbeat story about size 10 Judi, whose world spins out of control after she meets beauty queen Nancy Pratt, who gets her involved in the world of anorexia and bulimia.

QUICK PICKS

- FAT GIRL DANCES WITH ROCKS by Susan Stinson

- LIFE IN THE FAT LANE by Cherie Bennett

- MYRTLE OF WILLENDORF by Rebecca O'Connell

- THE CAT ATE MY GYMSUIT by Paula Danziger

Nonfiction

....

WAKE UP, I'M FAT by Camryn Manheim
Camryn Manheim's autobiography focuses on her struggle to succeed as a large-size actress.

....

BIG FAT LIES by Glenn A. Gaesser
Glenn Gaesser exposes the myth of the obesity epidemic.

....

NO FAT CHICKS: HOW BIG BUSINESS PROFITS BY MAKING WOMEN HATE THEIR BODIES — AND HOW TO FIGHT BACK by Terry Poulton
This wonderful exposé details Poulton's former life as a chronic dieter and how she tortured herself to lose sixty-five pounds in six months. Her personal story segues into what she calls the "billion-dollar brainwash," or how corporations, especially the diet and beauty industries, attempt to make women feel bad about themselves so they can increase their profit margin.

....

FAT! SO? BECAUSE YOU DON'T HAVE TO APOLOGIZE FOR YOUR SIZE by Marilyn Wann
Filled with stats, cartoons and quotes about dieting, fat humor, self-esteem and empowerment, Marilyn Wann's hilarious book is a shot in the arm to any fat person who needs to learn a little self-love. This was one of the books that put me on the road to fat acceptance.

LOSING IT by Laura Fraser
Laura Fraser blows the lid off the diet industry.

BOUNTIFUL WOMEN: LARGE WOMEN'S SECRETS FOR LIVING
THE LIFE THEY DESIRE by Bonnie Bernell and Carmen Renee Berry
Both a celebration and a how-to: affirming size while offering strategies
for handling challenging situations such as negotiating a tight squeeze on
an airplane or fielding judgmental comments.

FAT HISTORY: BODIES AND BEAUTY IN THE MODERN WEST by Peter Stearns
The volume explores the meaning of fat in contemporary Western society
and illustrates how cultural changes, such as the growth in consumer
culture, increasing equality for women, and the refocusing of women's
roles, have influenced today's obsession with fat.

FED UP by Terry Nicholetti Garrison
A well-researched book on the dangers and ineffectiveness of diets.

REAL WOMEN DON'T DIET by Ken Mayer
Photographer Mayer writes about being attracted to large-size women
and how he feels that they are unfairly targeted.

LEARNING CURVES: LIVING YOUR LIFE IN FULL AND WITH STYLE
by Michelle Weston
The fashion and style director of Mode, Weston shares her own story of
coming to terms with her size, along with the recollections of eight other
women, including model Kate Dillon and actress Kim Coles.

THE OBESITY MYTH: WHY AMERICA'S OBSESSION IS HAZARDOUS TO
YOUR HEALTH by Paul Campos
Close to half of the adult population is dieting, obsessed with achieving
an arbitrary "ideal weight." Yet studies show that a moderately active
larger person is likely to be far healthier (and likely to live longer) than
someone who is thin but sedentary. A provocative exposé of the culture
that thrives on the war on fat.

JUST THE WEIGHT YOU ARE: HOW TO BE FIT AND HEALTHY, WHATEVER
YOUR SIZE by Steven Jonas and Linda Konner
Steven Jonas, M.D., and fitness journalist Linda Konner assert that you
can get fit and healthy whatever your size. Includes profiles of fit, healthy
role models who weigh 300 pounds or more.

SELF-ESTEEM COMES IN ALL SIZES: HOW TO BE HAPPY AND HEALTHY
AT YOUR NATURAL WEIGHT by Carol Johnson
By separating physiological fact from popular fiction, Johnson helps
people understand that they are not always to blame for their size.

THE BIG GIRLS' GUIDE TO LIFE: A PLUS-SIZED JAUNT THROUGH
A BODY-OBSESSED WORLD by Bunkie Lynn.
A satirical look at the big girl's world. Teaches us to eat, to be happy, and
that chocolate does cure everything.

THE FAT GIRL'S GUIDE TO LIFE by Wendy Shanker
A very funny rant on being a big girl in a fat-hating world.

Resources

....

DANGEROUSLY CURVY NOVELS: *http://curvynovels.com*

If you are looking for an extensive list of novels with plus-size heroines, this is it. Dangerously Curvy Novels also has reviews, recommendations and reading lists.

Section 4: **Size-Positive Magazines and Zines**

According to a 2003 study in the *Journal of Adolescent Health*, reading fashion/beauty magazines can lower the self-esteem of young people. Fashion magazines offer unobtainable goals in thinness and "beauty" and often contradict themselves by running articles on anorexia and then featuring models who appear anorexic. As of now, it is very difficult to find size-positive magazines on the newsstands. *Radiance*, the biggest fat-positive magazine, stopped publishing a print version. Both *Mode* and *Grace Woman* have gone under, and *BBW* and *Dimensions* have sporadic publishing schedules. So in the meantime, enjoy some of the different online magazines and zines that are available.

....

ABUNDANCE MAGAZINE: *http://www.abundancemagazine.com*

Abundance Magazine is an online zine with articles, fiction, poetry and artwork. Has a very lively discussion board.

....

ADIOS BARBIE: *http://www.adiosbarbie.com*

Adios Barbie is a social-politic online journal about body acceptance. Although it goes beyond the topic of size, the site contains size-positive articles, interviews and information.

BBW MAGAZINE: *http://www.bbwmagazine.com*
Similar to other fashion magazines except everyone is pleasantly plump
and there is no talk of dieting. It offers plus-size women advice on beauty,
love and fashion. Although the magazine is currently on hiatus, when in
print it can be found at your local bookstore. In the meantime, enjoy the
Web site, which has articles from back issues.

DIMENSIONS: *http://www.dimensionsmagazine.com*
In print sporadically since 1984, this is a magazine for fat chicks and
their admirers. Although mostly concerning sexuality, erotic stories and
relationship connections for fat people, it also covers such subjects as
activism, health and medical issues.

EXTRA HIP (FOR TEENS): *http://www.extrahip.com*
This online teen magazine (originally launched in print) was created by
plus-size model Katie Arons and offers fashion tips, stories, and articles
on current trends, cute boys and what every teen should know about
plus-size modeling. Issues come out two to three times a year.

FIGURE: *http://www.figuremagazine.com*
A bimonthly women's magazine dedicated to full-figured women
(although many of the models in *Figure* seem to be size 10 to 16), *Figure* is
put out by Charming Shops, the same company that owns Lane Bryant,
Fashion Bug and Catherine's Plus Sizes. If you shop at any of these stores,
this magazine will feature the clothing you want, and more importantly,
coupons! Also, it offers beauty and fashion tips. However, a note of
warning here: there are some dieting ads.

GRAND WOMAN: *http://www.grandwoman.com*

This is a Canadian fashion magazine published bimonthly that is available in the United States by subscription only. It offers fashion and beauty tips for plus-size women and is geared mostly toward Canadians.

ON A POSITIVE NOTE:

http://www.largelypositive.com/Pages/Newsletter.html

The Official E-zine of Carol Johnson's Largely Positive comes out quarterly and is chock-full of subjects concerning fat chicks, such as style, self-esteem, health and weight discrimination.

RADIANCE: *http://www.radiancemagazine.com*

Radiance, like *Mode*, is defunct, but still has an online presence. On its Web site you can find selected fat-positive articles from previous issues.

RUBEN'S NEST: *http://www.theviproom.com/rubensnest*

Ruben's Nest is an online zine that first appeared in 1998. Unfortunately, due to time constraints, the two women who ran it stopped publishing in December 2001. But the site is still full of all the previous issues. Features a good list of plus-size shopping sites, and tips on fashion and dating.

SSBB WOMAN: *http://www.ssbbwoman.com*

SSBB Woman is an online magazine that comes out sporadically. The recent issue features an interview with a plus-size romance novelist, an article on NAAFA, poetry, a story about a designer for plus-size clothing, and more.

....

WITHOUT MEASURE (Official E-Zine of ISAA):

http://www.withoutmeasure.com

This official online magazine of the International Size Acceptance Association has come out two to three times annually since 2001. The site has interviews, activism tips, news and health features.

....

MODE MAGAZINE AND GRACE WOMAN

Unfortunately, these fashion magazines for larger women folded. You can still find old issues at used bookstores or on Ebay. *Mode* had fashion spreads, beauty tips and an advice column from Emme. It crashed after it was unable to consistently attract sufficient beauty advertisers. *Grace Woman* was started by the former editor of *Mode* and failed after seven issues when its main investor pulled out — despite the magazine having 200,000 subscribers.

"In department stores, the size 12 and 14 and 16 clothes are kept in a ghetto called the "Women's Department.""

SALLIE TISDALE

CHAPTER 4

SHOPPING IN THE THIN-CENTRIC WORLD

When I was 17, after years of being told by boys that I was a fat and ugly, one of them actually asked me to go to the high school prom with him. After about a week of floating on air and not quite believing he had actually asked *me*, I suddenly went into a panic at the realization that, oh my God, I needed to buy a prom dress. Since I was into punk music at the time, and generally wore all black like Darlene from *Roseanne*, my closet wasn't exactly filled with proper prom wear.

Not to worry. I went out with my mother, determined to find the perfect prom dress, preferably something that was puffy with black and white polka dots. However, after shopping at a multitude of department stores and finding absolutely nothing that fit me, I wound up buying a dress from a store for "big women." It had no puff, no sequins and was definitely not sexy. This taught me a valuable lesson at a young age — the fashion industry does not produce attractive clothes for fat women.

My many subsequent years of shopping have confirmed that teenage observation: *clothes for fat women are ugly*. Now, if you *want* to walk around looking like a tent, you'll love the selection out there. However, if you want to look cool, hip, or, heaven forbid, sexy, you are going to have a hard time shopping as a fat chick.

I want to make it a bit easier on you. So, as a favor to all my fat friends out there, I have spent the better part of a year braving the clothing stores of the USA in order to provide you with advice on the best and worst of what is out there.

First up are the major chain and department stores. Most of these stores can be found in Anywhere and Everywhere, USA. I've tried to review the major department and chains stores in order to tell you what to expect from each store in terms of style, location and sizing. Each review is based on at least two visits to each store, as well as an extensive view of what's available online.

A few tips before we get started. Remember that national chains can differ from region to region. What might be true in the Northeast, where I shopped, might not be true in Nebraska. I have also discovered in my research that many department stores hide the plus section on floors far away from the "normal" size clothing, or somewhere in the back of the store. The rule of thumb is that if it's hard to find, it's plus size.

Finally, a quick piece of advice from a fellow fat chick shopper — don't buy into the thinking that, "If it fits, it's good." The golden rule of shopping for fat or thin should be, "I will buy it only if it looks good on me."

Sizing

Plus size can start anywhere between sizes 12 and 18, depending on the store. When I was a size 16, I would find my size in both missus and plus size.

SIZE TERMS

JUNIORS

Clothing for older girls and teens. Typically runs in odd-numbered sizes from 0 to 13. It is rare to find big sizes for teens.

PETITE

Clothing for women with heights ranging from 4'8" to 5'4". I often find that petite can be easily defined as clothing for thin, short women. Typically, plus-size petites are found in the plus section and are labeled with "WP" for "women petite."

MISSUS, MISSY OR MISSES

Clothing for "regular" women with a height between 5'5" and 5'7". Typically includes even-numbered sizes from 0 to 12.

PLUS, WOMAN OR WOMEN

Clothing for larger women, cor-responding to a height of 5'5" to 5'8", usually even-numbered sizes 14 and upward.

TALL OR LONG

Clothing geared for tall women, usually located in the plus section.

Styles and Quantity

After visiting several stores, I became aware of a deadly style sickness — "Big Flower Syndrome" (BFS). In a trend that is almost exclusive to plus-size clothes, a giant flower is placed somewhere near the center of a shirt or top, in order to help hide the fat. It isn't always limited to flowers — sequins, gaudy colors, overabundance of buttons or bizarre patterns often serve the same purpose. Now, I'm not against fat women who want to wear bright, vibrant colors to stand out in the crowd, but it is important when you shop to be able to differentiate between "tasteful" and "tactless." When I judged styles, I always looked at the patterns to see whether or not they suffered from Big Flower Syndrome. It is a disease for which there is no cure, and which the fashion industry wants to inflict on the fat chick, so beware.

Section 1: **Chain Stores**

TARGET: *http://www.target.com*

Target offers affordable casuals and a small line of office clothes for petite, missus and plus. All the women's clothing is located in the same section. I found that missus was twice as big as plus, and missus sales items, maternity, and plus were often grouped together. To quote my assistant shopping buddy, Elle Snider, "Excuse me, I'm not pregnant!" Target's sizes go up to 24W and 3X, although I did not find all these sizes in the store on my two visits.

Using jeans as a price guide, I found plus size to be about 10 to 15 percent more expensive than missus. The jeans I saw did tend to be trendy and hip — I found a cute pair of Mossimo's. Elsewhere, I did see

Store Grades

A   A GREAT STORE FOR FAT CHICKS! IT HAS THE STYLES, SIZES, PRICES AND QUALITY THAT WILL MAKE A FAT CHICK HAPPY.

B   A GOOD STORE FOR FAT CHICKS. IT IS SOMEWHAT DEFICIENT IN SOME AREAS, BUT OVERALL, A RELIABLE PLACE FOR FAT CHICKS TO SHOP.

C   AN OK STORE FOR FAT CHICKS. IF YOU SPEND TIME LOOKING, YOU'LL PROBABLY FIND SOMETHING DECENT.

some "BFS" clothes — a perfect example was a black bathing suit with a long, large red stripe across the waist. The bra sizes go up to 48DD, underwear to 2X.

Online sizes go up to 24W, but not all sizes or styles were available. The plus-size section is only two Web pages in length, compared with over ten for missus (and three for maternity). *Grade:* **C+**

SEARS: *http://www.sears.com*

Sears' plus section is microscopic when compared with its other clothing sections. In one location that I visited, the missus section was extremely large, while the plus size was a small section of floor space tucked away in the back of the store. In other locations, the plus-size sections were found on the lower levels. On a positive note, Sears does have a Junior Plus section.

Most of the clothes feature very basic styles. However, they do carry Lands End. There were some big flowers mixed throughout, but there were also a good deal of solids. Jeans run about $30, casual T-shirts range from $10 to $25, dresses anywhere from $30 to $100. The cost of plus-size clothes is only about 5 percent higher than missus clothes. Bras go up to 44DD and underwear to size 10. Sears carries plus-size coats in the winter, as well as some plus-size petites. Their biggest size is 26, but it is difficult to find.

Online, Sears offers sizes up to34W and 5X, but the clothing is modeled by thin women. *Grade:* **B-**

....

WAL-MART: *http://www.walmart.com*

The Wal-Mart clothing section is complete size chaos. While the signs in its stores say it has up to size 28W, in one store I found 32W, and in another, only up to 24W. In addition, plus size and missus were mixed together in some stores, and separate in others.

The size I found the most was 22W. It has petite and tall sizes, but I could find them only up to size 18. Bathing suits go up to 3X and 22W. Underwear goes to size 14 and bras to size 44D and 42DD, but in one location I found a 48DD. Also, Wal-Mart has up to 2XL in sleepwear.

I often found bigger sizes near the bottom of the pile, especially among blue jeans and underwear. Bobby Brook pants and shirts are about $3 more for plus size, compared with missus. I found Faded Glory pants at $18.87 in plus size, $15.92 in missus.

Wal-Mart's selection of clothes is stylish, generally solid in color, and tasteful for business wear. However, Big Flower Syndrome and large patterns dominate casual wear. Wal-Mart carries a brand called "George Woman" that look like it was made in the 1970s. There are some trendy, cute clothes in big sizes, including flowing blouses with "India" patterns, NASCAR T-shirts and stretch jeans. However, if you want to find something chic, you gotta dig. Thankfully, in its ads, Wal-Mart uses large models.

It recently added an online apparel section, which is extremely limited in selection. *Grade:* **B**

....

MACY'S: *http://www.macys.com*
Macy's has a separate section for plus-size women, which is called "Macy's Woman." This department is usually quarantined on the top floor away from the other clothes, and is also smaller than the others women's departments. Macy's Woman sizes go up to 24 and prices are about 5 percent more than for missus. They offered a few petite plus sizes.

The colors were generally solid, but seemed geared toward older women. However, clothing on their Web site is designed for a much younger demographic, with items such as jean jackets, belly button shirts and cargo pants. If, like me, you want to wear trendy clothes, it is best to shop online at Macy's. They feature plus-size models in their ads.

The bra sizes go up to sizes 50DDD and 12/3X in underwear, but a good portion of the underwear is something called "Slenderizers." Online, they offer up to size 24/3X. Macy's is a good store if you're looking for a wide variety of styles and sizes, but: *Grade:* **B+**

OLD NAVY: *http://www.oldnavy.com*

If you like denim and lots of up-to-the-minute fashions, Old Navy is the place to go. It specializes in chic urban fashions and casuals, and it carries up to size 26 both in its stores and online. Some of the highlights are low-rise jeans ($34), or denim trousers ($36) for a dressier look. Thongs go up to size 3X. About 60 percent of the plus line is the same as the missus line, while the remainder is specially designed. Online, it celebrates the plus-size look, with quotes such as, "This is the best time to be a Plus-Sized woman," and a testimonial from Abby, the chain's online plus-size model, who exclaims with glee, "I don't want to hide my curves. I love my curves." Probably the best chain store for fat chicks to find something stylish and sexy. *Grade:* **A**

LORD AND TAYLOR: *http://www.lordandtaylor.com*

Lord and Taylor is an upscale clothing store offering everything from casuals to formalwear. Sizes range from 14 to 24/3X, but I found mostly sizes 20 and 22 in the stores I visited. Bras go up to size 42DDD and underwear to XL/10, but on one visit I did find a 14/15.

Although its styles tend to run conservative, it features lots of solid colors and unobtrusive patterns. It carries designer clothes from Jones NY, Liz Claiborne, etc. Plus-size clothes are about 15 percent more than missus in the store, but all clothes cost the same in the sales catalog. The plus sections are usually on a different floor than missus and are about half the size. They had no clothes available online, although you can view the sales catalog. Lord and Taylor is good for style, but little else. *Grade:* **C+**

JC PENNEY: *http://www.jcpenney.com*

JC Penney is a moderate to inexpensive department store that offers everything from casual to semiformal clothing. Sadly, the plus sections I visited were messy and disorganized, and the clothes themselves not very stylish (think things that your grandmother would love!). And, prices are about 10 to 15 percent higher than for missus.

JC Penney sizes go up to size 24/ 3X, though I did find a size 26 in one store and a size 28 in another. The plus size sections are well hidden, and when you find them, you will discover that they occupy much less floor space than missus or petite. The biggest size bra I found was 40F. Most "full figured" bras were 36 to 44DD and it seemed that the larger the bra, the simpler the style.

JC Penney has featured a Junior Plus section for the past ten years. This section does feature some cute clothes such as Levi Jeans and trendy tops like ponchos and wrap sweaters, but, unfortunately, the selection is limited. Online the size chart went up to 32, but I couldn't find anything bigger than 3X (24 to 26). JC Penney does have plus-size mannequins and plus-size models in ads. *Grade:* **B**

KOHL'S: *http://www.kohls.com*

Overall, Kohl's styles are very bland and basic. The colors and patterns are not eye-catching, but on the positive side, I didn't see much Big Flower Syndrome. Its plus size seems geared overwhelming to the matronly, older woman. For price comparison, I looked at designers such as Sag Harbor, Gloria Vanderbilt and Erika, and didn't find more than a 5-percent difference from missus.

Although Kohl's plus section isn't microscopic in size when compared with the missus department, it is usually tucked way in the back, far from prying, thin eyes, I guess. Its biggest size is 24/3X. Bra sizes go up to 42DDD, size 11 for underwear, but the larger the size, the less there is of them in the store. And, while there was plenty of sexy underwear in the missus section, the plus section was dominated by granny panties. There is sleepwear that goes up to 3X. Online, Kohl's offers a better selection of plus-size clothing. Overall, the sizes and styles in the plus-size section are very limited for the younger, hipper, not gray-haired shopper. *Grade:* **B-**

....

NORDSTROM: *http://www.nordstrom.com*
The plus section, which is called "Encore," is listed under "Special Sizes." It is often found next to the petites department, yet, in one location, a designer missus section had somehow wandered its way into its center. (One hopes this was due to construction that was going on in the store.) Sizes run to 24, but I found mostly 16, 18 and 22. It has a variety of styles, offering causal, business, semiformal and formal, and carries designer clothes like Dana Buchman and Lauren. I was pleased to see some very sexy dresses, including some with v-neck shirts, and skirts that hit just below the knee. It also offers shoes up to size 14 in single and double width, and wide-calf boots. Bras go up to size 40F, 36G and 42D, and underwear to size 15. Overall, prices are similar to missus, but I found a Misook jacket that cost $60 more than one in missus. The department features larger size mannequins.

If you can afford more expensive clothes and are looking for a one-stop shop, a wealthy fat chick could do worse than Nordstrom. *Grade:* **B+**

BLOOMINGDALE'S: *http://www.bloomingdales.com*

Bloomingdale's plus-size department is usually located in the basement, along with the housewares. The main store in New York City has the plus section in the sub-basement, where I could touch the ceiling and couldn't get a signal on my cell phone. Maybe one day they'll move the department out of the dungeon.

The department takes up one-third of the floor space of missus and petite. There are sizes from 14 to 24, and I did find a wide variety. While Bloomingdale's carries some stylish T-shirts, most of the clothes are geared toward older women. Even the supposedly "sexy" clothes feature some extremely painful patterns (BFS alert!). They do carry formalwear, although it is mostly for the matronly shopper (but I did find a few sleeveless dresses). Bras and underwear are pathetic — they go up to 36DDD and 42D, underwear only to size 9. And, the models in the plus section are thin! For price comparison, I found a Jones NY jacket in missus for $199, or $219 for plus size.

A few plus sizes are listed on its Web site, but some serious search time is required, because not all outfits include plus sizes. *Grade:* **C-**

SAKS FIFTH AVENUE: *http://www.saksfifthavenue.com*

Saks' plus-size section is called "Salon Z." At least the name sounds cool; I can't say the same for the clothes. While missus clothes are slick and sexy, plus-size stuff is homey and "colorful." In other words, Big Flower Syndrome has struck Salon Z. In addition, they do not have a wide variety of formalwear, only a few dresses that my grandmother would love. The sizes in Salon Z range from 14 to 24

Clothing prices for plus size are much more expensive than for missus. An Anne Klein jacket cost $375 in missus, $525 in plus, a Dana Buchman white jacket $388 in missus, $448 in plus. They now carry plus-size fur, for all you Zsa Zsa Gabor fans.

Saks does have a very impressive bra selection, with sizes up to 36G and 40F. However, the largest size I could find in underwear was seven, although one store did have a few token 10's. I suspect, but can't prove, that the underwear section is designed for thin women who have had boob jobs.

One of the most exciting parts of shopping at Saks is trying to find what floor Salon Z is on. The answer is either the top floor or the basement. Online, they have a much better selection. However, the majority of Salon Z clothes are modeled by thin women. *Grade:* **C**

....

FASHION BUG: *http://fashionbug.charmingshoppes.com/homefb.asp*
Owned by Charming Shoppes, which is the parent company of Lane Bryant and Catherine Plus Size, Fashion Bug is geared toward a twenty- to thirtysomething crowd and is an excellent store for casual clothing, with a fat-chick-friendly atmosphere thrown in! An example of this atmosphere — it is the only store I visited where the plus section is bigger than the missus section.

It carries up to size 30/4X, although it has a better selection in the smaller plus sizes. Missus was a little more chic than plus, but overall, the styles were fairly similar. I did spot a few pieces suffering from Big Flower Syndrome, but there were lots of pretty denim skirts, capris and pants to make up for it.

It recently started selling clothing from its Web site, where it offers a wide variety of styles and sizes, including coats and shoes. *Grade:* **B+**

DOTS: *http://www.dots.com*

Dots is a hip and stylish store geared toward girls, teens and young adults. Plus sizes run from 14 to 24/3X, but most of the clothes I found were 16 and 2X. Style wise, the missus and plus sections are similar, except for a few more cases of Big Flower Syndrome in plus size. Overall, though, colors and patterns were tastefully put together, and there were many solid colors and pinstripes. The plus section seems to feature more causalwear than the missus, which has a larger selection of professional wear. One location featured tank tops for women with big breast sizes. Bras go up to size 42DD and underwear to size 9. The plus section has some chubby mannequins.

Prices seem comparable, but it's hard to differentiate since missus and plus do not carry the same brands. However, jeans in both sections were around $20. Dots sells no clothes online. *Grade:* **A-**

NEWPORT NEWS: *http://www.newport-news.com*

Newport News is an online clothing store and print catalog that offers plus, petite and tall under "Special Sizes." They carry casuals, swimwear, businesswear, sleepwear and outerwear. Pantsuits are priced around $90, pants about $50, with plus size about 10 percent more spendy than missus. Missus clothes are often available in plus and go up to size 24W, with selected items going to 26W. The models appeared to be smaller than a size 12, but there are solid, vibrant colors -- absolutely no sign of big flowers. They also have very sexy dresses, even some with spaghetti straps to show off those shoulders! *Grade:* **B+**

Specialty

FREDERICK'S OF HOLLYWOOD: *http://www.fredericks.com*
Frederick's of Hollywood carries large size bras, sexy underwear and teddies up to size 3X. The selection isn't very good — they have more clothes for smaller women than large. However, they do acknowledge that some plus-size women buy sexy underwear, as they have up to size 42F in bras and size 2X underwear. But, the bigger the bra, the less sexy it is. In their stores, Frederick's has a pink label on the hanger to indicate plus sizes. There isn't a price differences between petite, missus and plus. Online, sizes go up to 24 and 3X. They do not have plus-size women modeling their clothes. *Grade:* **B-**

DAVID'S BRIDAL: *http://www.www.davidsbridal.com*
David's Bridal carries all variety of wedding dresses up to size 26. The plus section features thirteen different dress styles made exclusively for sizes 14 to 26. However, the majority of the collection goes to only size 20, and bridesmaid dresses go to size 24. There are no price differences until size 20, when the bill goes up about 10 percent. It also carries Oleg Cassini, though those dresses are 20 percent more after size 16. As a veteran of buying bridesmaid and wedding dresses, I can tell you that David's Bridal sizes tend to run small, so beware. *Grade:* **B-**

Honorable mentions

- CHADWICKS goes to size 26 on selective clothes.
  http://www.chadwicks.com

- COLDWATER CREEK goes up to 22/3X and online to size 26. There is more of a selection online and in the print catalog.
  http://www.coldwatercreek.com

- EDDIE BAUER goes to size 26 on selected clothes.
  http://www.eddiebauer.com

- H&M carries large-size clothes in small ghettos in eleven of their stores in the Northeast, Virginia and Illinois. *http://www.hm.com*

- NEIMAN MARCUS carries plus-size clothing up to size 28 only in their catalog and online. *http://www.neimanmarcus.com*

- DILLARD'S goes to size 3X and 24W. *http://www.dillards.com*

- KAUFMANN'S carries business, casual and semiformal to size 24W/3X, bras to 46DDD and underwear to size 12.
  http://www.kaufmanns.com

Section 2: **Stores Built for Fat Chicks**

This section reviews stores that are designed specifically for fat chicks. While department and chain stores are moving forward in terms of catering to larger-sized women, most don't (yet) have the range of styles or sizes to compete with stores specifically geared toward them.

....

DRESS BARN WOMEN: *www.dressbarn.com*

Dress Barn is an upscale clothing store that offers a variety of women's clothes ranging from causal to semiformal. Its plus-size version, Dress Barn Women, is often located right next door. Featuring a separate section for plus and missus, Dress Barn Women goes up to size 24 and offers a nice mix of business and casualwear in mostly solid colors. Beware, though, that it does carry a few items infected with fatal Big Flower Syndrome, including one dress that I will kindly call a "burlap sack with flowers."

Plus size is about 10 percent more expensive than the other clothing, and Dress Barn Women is more expensive than other clothing stores such as Target and JC Penney. A semi-casual dress costs about $80, for example. You can't order online, but you can browse the latest fashions and sales. *Grade:* **B+**

....

ELISABETH BY LIZ CLAIBORNE: *http://www.elisabeth.com*

Plus-size clothes by designer Liz Claiborne go up to size 24W and include a relatively large section for petite plus size. The majority of the clothes are geared toward older women, with a good portion of business casual wear. About 50 percent are solids with unobtrusive patterns, though the rest suffer from a tendency toward flora-covered pieces — I was bewildered by flower-patterned corduroy pants. The prices range from $29 for a long-sleeve T-shirt, to $65 for a denim skirt, to $199 for a wool jacket. And, the mannequins are fat! They offer more quantity online, where you can find a virtual sales rack. *Grade:* **B**

....

LANE BRYANT: *http://www.lanebryant.com*
A longtime shopper of Lane Bryant, I find their clothes have been typically geared toward older women with a "cover-up" style. But, in the past few years, they are featuring more clothing for young women who want to show off their curves. I saw a cute mesh cami ($24), a shimmery poncho ($49), and a short black stretch skirt with a ruffled hem ($34). This is also the place to get fashionable jeans — it carries a low-rise stretch flare jean ($39.50) and Glamour Magazine's favorite, the stretch bootcut. Sizes range up to 28, and it features plus-size models from modeling agencies Ford 12 Plus and Wilhelmina Plus in its ads. It also carries lingerie (I spied a cute lacy thong) and accessories. *Grade:* **A-**

....

THE AVENUE: *http://www.avenue.com*
The Avenue is a less expensive version of Lane Bryant, but with bigger sizes. It offers a great range of casualwear, businesswear, undergarments, sleepwear and nightlife outfits up to size 32. Many of the clothes are also made for petite and tall women. The styles are attractive, with solid colors and tasteful patterns, although there were a few dresses with floral patterns. Prices are relatively inexpensive — jeans for $49 and blouses from $39 to $59. The ads feature plus-size models, but in one of the stores I saw an image of a half-naked thin woman advertising underwear. The Web site has a much better selection, but beware — it is littered

with thin women modeling the underwear. Bras go up to size 44DD and 42DDD and underwear goes up to size 32. It also has a nice line of accessories — I especially liked the leather tote bags. *Grade:* **B+**

CATHERINE'S PLUS SIZES: *http://www.catherines.com*

As I entered Catherine's Plus Sizes, I was assaulted by a giant red flower on the front of a cream blouse. All I could think was that if someone were wearing that shirt, her weight would be the second thing anyone would notice. Thankfully, the rest of the clothes weren't as horrific, although they seemed geared toward older women.

Catherine's carries Liz and Me, a new line of stylish clothing for hard-to-fit bodies, which it designed by examining 3,000 plus-size women in order to make the size determinations. It has a great selection of suits, sleepwear, and casuals, and also large-size stockings and accessories. Businesswear is tasteful, conservative and features patterns that don't look like a train wreck of color. The muumuus are in the basement with the bras, underwear and more formal dresses. There is a greater mix of style online.

While Catherine's is mixed on style, it is superb on sizes. Of all the plus-size chain stores, Catherine's carries the biggest sizes — up to 38, and I found a large selection of every size. Bras go up to an impressive size 54, but the cup size only goes to DDD. Prices range from $30 to $100, and dress suits from $40 to $75; and blouses and pants start at $30. They feature large women in their ads. *Grade:* **A-**

TALBOTS WOMAN: *http://www.talbots.com*

Talbots Woman is a fairly expensive store that offers conservative casual and business wear. It has up to size 24W/3X and plus-size petites. The size I found the most of was 18, although there were a few 24's and lots of size 12's. (If you are a 12, you shouldn't have a problem finding clothes in missus.) Clothing prices are expensive — suits are around $270, dresses $150, skirts between $100 and $150, blouses $70. (I was saved by the large sale rack.) It also has large-size accessories, where I noticed some very fine leather belts, handbags and gloves. Talbots Woman is also the queen of solid colors, though the styles are suited for your local country club. Online, there is more selection, but those prices! *Grade:* **B-**

ASHLEY STEWART WOMAN: *http://www.ashleystewart.com*

Plus-size stores should take note of Ashley Stewart. This clothing store is geared to full-figured African-American women and it creates an atmosphere that makes you feel like a queen. It sells jeans, dresses, sweat suits, pajamas and large-size accessories, including hosiery, hats and gloves. Sizes range from 14 to 26, and there is a variety in each size. Though they carry styles for a variety of ages, many are geared toward older women. Not much Big Flower Syndrome here, although there were some shiny flora blouses tucked in a corner. Underwear goes up to 12 and bras to size 44DD, 46D. Prices are reasonable — $10 for tank tops, $29 for jeans, and tops and blouses around $20. You can't order online, but you can look at the clothes and the latest video. *Grade:* **A-**

Teens/Young Adults

TORRID: *http://www.torrid.com*

Torrid is a breath of fresh air in the plus-size world. While adult fat women have the luxury of Lane Bryant, Elizabeth, Catherine's Plus Sizes and the Avenue, fat teens and young women are often left in the dust. Luckily there is Torrid, which is geared toward young women and teens who want funky, punk, gothic and chic clothes. It offers dresses, including prom dresses, skirts, pants, wide-calf and large-size ankle boots, belts, chokers and other accessories. It also has a lot of clothes with kid-style fun — prints such as fairies, Hello Kitty and Cat in the Hat. During Halloween season it carries sexy costumes in large sizes. It also features designers like Z Cavaricci, Paris Blues, Dickies, Dollhouse, and clothes from boutique vendors like Tripp and Lip Service.

It is a little expensive for causal clothes, which can range from $20 to $100, but it has a great sale rack. You'll find sizes 12 to 26 or 4X, and a good amount of each. There are big mannequins, and most of their saleswomen don't look like Barbie. In fact, the store uses its own employees as its models.

Hot Topic, Torrid's parent company, is opening new stores every year, and CEO Elizabeth "Betsy" McLaughlin is a big, beautiful chick. Stores are currently located in 22 states, and if you aren't in these states, you can order online, where you'll find a virtual sales rack. *Grade:* **A**

Online Stores

A word of caution when shopping online: Online stores are great for large-size women, but make sure items are returnable, since clothes that look good on the Web may not look good on your body.

....

JUST MY SIZE: *http://www.justmysize.com*

Though Just My Size offers businesswear, casuals, undergarments, dresses, sleepwear, bathing suits and hosiery, it is famous for underwear, which goes up to size 14, bras to 52FF. A good portion of the underwear offered is control-top. For the rest of the clothes, sizes vary from product to product, but it carries up to 6X (size 40). However, the clothes are expensive — $79 for a casual business suit — and the styles are bland and tired (think 1992). My recommendation: Skip the clothes, and go for what goes under them. They have two physical locations, in Massachusetts and Texas, with plans for expansion. *Grade:* **B-**

....

ALIGHT: *http://www.alight.com*

The first thing you think of when you to Alight's Web site is variety. It carries sweaters, dresses, tops, jeans and some bras and underwear. The style is hip, chic and cute — designs by FUBU and Emme, babydoll dresses, and bustier tops for all the cleavage-baring women — and there are lots of solid colors and sexy patterns, with no trace of Big Flower Syndrome. This is the best online store to buy up-to-the-minute styles.

Sizes are confusing. And although the Web site said Alight carried sizes from 14 to 28, I found up to a 32 (though most things ranged from 1X to 3X). Dresses ranged from $100 to $200, knit tops from $15 to $40, and jeans from $40 to $60. The models were a mixture of fat and thin. *Grade:* **A**

B&LU: *http://www.bandlu.com*

A plus store geared to teens and young adults, B&Lu carries clothes that range from causal to semi-causal, including jeans, pants, dresses and underwear. Style-wise, much of their stuff is chic and sexy, with kimono tops, sleeveless shirts, cool jerseys and some short, skimpy dresses and skirts. Sizes range from 14 to 24. Things are a little pricey, with jeans at $40, shorts $20, tops from $20 to $30, and dresses around $40. There is an online sales rack. Some of the clothes are modeled by large-size women. *Grade:* **A-**

ZAFTIQUE: *http://www.zaftique.com*

Zaftique carries it all: casual, dressy, lingerie, swimsuits and outerwear. Much of the stuff is stylish and sexy, although there is some stuff that can frighten, such as the "Mardi Gras tank top" and a gold floral dress that made me question my existence. Zaftique is very impressive in the size department, ranging to 8X. However, it is moderately expensive, with dresses from $50 to $90, shirts from $30 to $60, and pants from $30 to $60. It carries lingerie, but no bras. All the models are big. My advice — stick with the dressier stuff. *Grade:* **B**

MAKING IT BIG: *http://www.makingitbigonline.com*

Making It Big offers shorts, shirts, pants, dresses, shoes, intimates and bathing suits. Sizes start at 16W and run to an impressive 44W. It uses a different sizing system, XS=3X, and 1 is really a 16, so check the sizing chart before you order. Prices are about the same as other plus stores, dresses around $60, pants about $50. The clothing is plain and matronly — the cover-up-thy-fat look is all the rage here. And, when I visited the Web site, the spotlight swimsuit was covered with — what else? — big flowers. All the models are big. Making It Big has a bricks-and-mortar store in California. *Grade:* **B-**

....

MYLES AHEAD: *http://www.mylesahead.com*
Myles Ahead caters to supersized Goddess women, with sizes that range up to 10X. It carries clothes that are casual, business, formal and dressy. Most are long, flowing and not very sexy, but the colors are vibrant and tasteful. There is a smattering of Big Flower Syndrome, but it isn't widespread. The clothes are on the expensive side — a black dress with matching jacket was $200. The virtual sales rack offers up to $30 off the original price. Myles Ahead has a retail store in Florida. *Grade:* **B**

....

KIYONNA: *http://www.kiyonna.com*
Kiyonna designs can be found in boutiques all over the country, as well as on its Web site. Its style is chic and urban, with lots of v-necks, short skirts and sleeveless dresses. It uses plus-size models, and sizes go up to 5X. The store currently has six collections and recently launched a lingerie line. Dresses range from $100 to $150, blouses from $40 to $70, and skirts from $45 to $60. Kiyonna also runs an online lingerie store — *http://www.alectra.com* — that has sexy underwear up to size 4X, but the models in the underwear are thin. *Grade:* **A-**

....

THE BIG, THE BAD AND THE BEAUTIFUL: *http://www.bigbadbeautiful.com*
This store's sizes range from petite to goddess, but I would recommend looking at the size chart to gauge where you fit on its scale. It also offers "super sizes" and customized clothing to fit any size, and styles for

formal, casual, work and lingerie. There are no hideous patterns or drab colors, but overall, the clothing is on the plain side. Two-piece sets are its specialties, and the prices ranged from $100 for a purple velvet pantsuit to $190 for a jacket and matching dress. The Web site is very fat-positive and all the models look like your next-door fat chick. The Big, the Bad and the Beautiful has a physical store in California. *Grade:* **A-**

Specialty Stores

PLUS-SIZE BRIDAL: *http://www.plussizebridal.com*
In addition to bridal dresses, this store offers prom dresses, bridal undergarments and shoes. Sizes range from 16 to 32. Prices range from $200 to $600, which is inexpensive for a wedding dress. The Web site featured several beautiful gowns in halter-top, strapless, off the shoulder, and long-sleeved styles. The designs were tasteful, not overly ornate. Models are chubby to mid-size in range. You will definitely not feel like a giant cream puff on your wedding day in these dresses! *Grade:* **A**

SYDNEY'S CLOSET: *http://www.sydneyscloset.com*
Sydney's Closet is a rarity in that it carries only plus-size formal wear. The dresses run the gamut of every formal event in a fat chick's life — prom, homecoming, wedding, etc. Everything is stylish and sexy and looks very much like the stuff you see in your typical missus section. (Many are strapless or have spaghetti straps. I wish I'd had this option when I was shopping for my prom dress.) Sizes range from 14 to 44. Sadly, I found some thin models on the Web site. (Fat chicks want to see same-size models to know how the dress will really look when we put it on.) Prices range from $150 to $300. *Grade:* **A**

ALWAYS FOR ME: *http://www.alwaysforme.com*

Always For Me sells mostly swimwear and underwear, with a smattering of dresses mixed in. Most items go up to size 20, but there were a few 24's. The swimsuits are cute, with lots of tankinis, swim-dresses, and tasteful one-pieces, and ranged in price from $50 to $124. The dresses ran from $160 to $300. It also carries plus-size Danskin wear and Delta Burke Yoga Tops for you workout fanatics. Full-figured bras run up to size 42DD and were priced from $20 to $30, and you'll find underwear up to size 4X. Many of the models are chunky, but not really fat. Always For Me has a physical location in Illinois. *Grade:* **B+**

AUDRADELLA'S PLUS-SIZE FASHIONS: *http://www.audradella.com*

Audradella's offers swimwear and intimates, with sizes that range from 16 to 26/3X, although not everything is available at all sizes. If you have a big bust, it's a good place to get a bikini, as there are tops here that run up to a size G cup. Additionally, the swimwear is made to order and cut on exact measurements. Bras go to 44DD and are in the $30 price range, corsets in the $70 range. All clothes are in solid colors, and everything I have bought from them lies nicely. The models are chubby but not very fat. *Grade:* **A-**

Other online stores

ASTARTE: *http://www.astartewoman.com*
Sleek urban looks. Custom made up to 77" busts and 90" hips.

A BIG ATTITUDE: *http://www.abigattitude.com*
Workout clothing up to 6X.

BIG GIRL GEAR: *http://www.biggirlgear.com*
Sparkly designs up to 77" busts and 90" hips.

BIGGER BRAS: *http://www.biggerbras.com*
Many choices here. Sizes go up to 56DD/F/G.

DAPHNE: *http://www.daphne1.com/catalog.php*
Simple, loose, flowing clothing in sizes up to 5X.

JESSICA LONDON: *http://www.jessicalondon.com*
Conservative career and casual wear in sizes up to 34W.

JUNONIA: *http://www.junonia.com*
Active and casual wear in sizes up to 4X.

PEGGY LUTZ: *http://www.plus-size.com*
Trend-setting plus-size couture in sizes up to 38/40. Kathy Bates wore one of their designs in About Schmidt.

PERSEPHONE: *http://www.persopheneplus.com*

Custom-made gothic dresses. http://www.persephoneplus.com

PLUS WOMAN: *http://www.pluswoman.com*

Custom made to order sizes up to 10X. Also carries plus-size medical scrubs.

ROAMANS: *http://www.roamans.com*

Casual, business, formal and lingerie in sizes up to 6X. Warning, Will Robinson: Heavily infected with Big Flower Syndrome!

SILHOUETTES: *http://www.silhouettes.com*

Casual and business wear in sizes up to 7X. If loose tunics are what you're looking for, shop here.

SIZE APPEAL: *http://www.sizeappeal.com*

Their slogan is, "Be Bold and Sexy Because You Can," and they mean it. Sexy clothes in sizes up to 3X.

Plus-Size Designers

DELTA BURKE REAL SIZE COLLECTIONS: *http://www.realsize.com*

ULLA POPKEN: *http://www.ullapopken.com*

KEY GARNER: *http://www.keygarner.com*

JULIE BENAC: *http://www.juliebenacdesigns.com*

DANA BUCHMAN WOMAN: *http://www.danabuchman.com*

TUESDAY CONNER: *http://www.tuesdayconner.com*

Plus-Size Clothing Resources

BOOKS

LIFE IS NOT A DRESS SIZE: RITA FARRO'S GUIDE TO ATTITUDE, STYLE, AND A NEW YOU, by Rita Faro

PLUS STYLE: THE PLUS-SIZE GUIDE TO LOOKING GREAT, by Suzan Nanfeldt

SIZING UP: FASHION FITNESS AND SELF-ESTEEM FOR FULL FIGURED WOMEN, by Sandy Summers Head

WEB SITES

ELEGANT PLUS: *http://www.elegantplus.com*
This site is a portal to all things fashion and style in the plus-size world.

PLUS-SIZE BRA: *http://www.plussizebras.org*
You won't find plus-size bras at this site, but you will find a guide to finding a bra in the right size.

PLUS-SIZE LIVING: *http://www.plussizeliving.com*

PLUS-SIZE FASHION MALL: *http://www.fashionplussize.com*

"We all know that many Americans are 'overweight' or 'clinically obese' from media reports."

CHAPTER 5

PLANES, TRAINS & AUTOMOBILES:
Seating Issues for Fat Chicks

F inding a proper size seat is an issue that large people face on an everyday basis. There is nothing more embarrassing than being in a public place — an airplane, a bus, a movie theater, a restaurant — and finding that the seats are not designed with you and your size in mind. While I will admit that things have improved a bit over the past few years — in New York City, where I live, newer subway cars use bench seats that don't have a clearly delineated seating area — the typical seat in America is not designed for the typical fat person in America.

One of the worst offenders of seating discrimination is the airline industry. In order to make as much money as possible, airlines try to cram as many people as possible into an airplane, resulting in seats that are too small for even the average-size thin person. And, while only Southwest has an official policy that forces you to buy an extra seat if you cannot fit into one seat (a policy they are currently being sued for as this book goes to press), many other airlines will put pressure on a fat person to buy a second seat. In addition, as I was finishing up this book, the airline industry had the nerve to say that the increasing weight of Americans is responsible for higher fuel costs on airplanes.

The problem is not just limited to airplanes and public places. Even things that we own are not designed for us, the owners. A friend of mine recently purchased a Honda Odyssey but found that she could not fit comfortably into the driver's seat when wearing her seat belt. When she asked Honda for seat belt extenders, she was told they were "not available at the present time." She ended up cutting the seat belt in the back and sewing it on to the front so it would be long enough.

Now, I want you to be as comfortable as possible while reading my book, so the following information on seating policies and requirements should help you to make informed choices when traveling, eating out, or buying a car. So, sit back (yes, you can put your feet up) and enjoy.

Buying a Car: A Handy Checklist

SEATING — Check the following: How far back do the seats go? Do you have enough stomach room in front? Is there enough room in the backseat for a passenger? (Bring an extra person on the test drive so that person can try out the back.) If backseats aren't a priority, look at two-door cars; they are easier to enter. Keep in mind that bench seats tend to provide more space than bucket seats.

LOAD CAPACITY AND SUSPENSION — This aspect controls how much weight the vehicle can handle. *Consumer Reports* lists the best and worst load capacity vehicles. Make sure the car can handle you, your friends and your stuff!

HEADROOM — Having more headroom also makes it easier to get out of the car. Make sure you can lower the seats if you have to.

STEERING WHEEL — Newer vehicles allow the driver to move the steering wheel up and down. Once you have the steering wheel in a comfortable spot for driving, make sure it is at a comfortable level for exiting and entering the vehicle. You don't want to adjust the steering wheel every time you get in and out of the car.

ERGONOMICS — Can you easily reach all the controls in the car? The windows, locks, gears, mirror? If you have trouble reaching the lever to move the seat, you may want to invest in motorized seats (although the mechanism for motorized seats will decrease headroom), or in a car that has a lever on the side.

SEAT BELT EXTENDERS — Seat belts are required in 49 states, yet they are only required to fit a person weighing up to 215 pounds. Seat belt extenders add about five inches to the length of the belt. When you get into a car, try the seat belt to see if it fits and is comfortable. If you need to, ask for an extender (and make sure that fits comfortably as well).

....

THE FOLLOWING COMPANIES OFFER SEAT BELT EXTENDERS FOR FREE:
Buick, Cadillac, Chevrolet, Chrysler, Dodge, Ford, GMC, Infiniti, Jeep, Lexus, Mazda, Mitsubishi, Nissan, Oldsmobile, Plymouth, Pontiac, Saab, Toyota, Volvo

....
THE FOLLOWING COMPANIES CHARGE ADDITIONAL MONEY FOR
SEAT BELT EXTENDERS:

Mercedes-Benz, Saturn, Subaru, Suzuki, Volkswagen

....
THE FOLLOWING COMPANIES DO NOT OFFER SEAT BELT EXTENDERS:

Acura, Audi, Hyundai, Kia, Porsche, Honda America

....
THE FOLLOWING COMPANIES OFFER CUSTOMIZED LONGER SEAT BELTS:

Jaguar, BMW, Land Rover

....
COMFY CARS FOR FAT CHICKS:

Plymouth Breeze, Dodge Ram, Honda Element, Chevy S10 Pickup, GMC Serria truck, Dodge Neon Malibu LS, Nissan Micra, VW Golf, Chevy Cavalier, Plymouth Voyager, Jeep Grand Cherokee, Mercury Topaz, Buick Lesabre, Chevy S-10, Land Rover, Suburban, Saturn SL1, Chevy Malibu LS, GMC Sonoma, Aztec, Dodge Caravan, VW Jetta, Nissan Sentra, Chevy Corsica

The plane ride <u>not</u> from hell: Comfort in the skies

- CALL AHEAD. If you think you will need an extra seat, call ahead and book the extra seat. All airlines are supposed to have seat belt extenders on their airplanes, but they often don't. If you don't want to worry about the seat belt extender, you can buy your own from Amplestuff: *www.amplestuff.com.*

- WHICH SEAT SHOULD YOU PICK? Go for a window or aisle seat. If you are in the middle, you are more likely to get squashed between two people. If you're on a plane with five seats in the center, and two on each side, go for the inside aisle. If you can afford it, fly first class or business class. The seats tend to be bigger and roomier. If you can't afford first class, be sure to check online or by phone to see what the seat dimensions are on your flight.

- **WHAT TIME SHOULD YOU LEAVE?** Always attempt to leave during off-peak hours, which will increase the chances of there being an empty seat next to you.

- **MAKING THE FLIGHT MORE FAT-FRIENDLY.** You might want to consider bringing a briefcase to use as a tray if the tray table does not fit over you. Don't feel uncomfortable asking the person in front of you to move up during mealtimes. If you are goddess-size, you should pre-board. Aisles are narrow and it will be easier to get yourself seated and comfortable if the plane is mostly empty. Be sure to put the armrest up as soon as possible. Use the restroom before you board so there is less of a chance you'll have to squeeze into the miniature restroom on the plane.

- **WHAT TO DO IF YOU HAVE A PROBLEM...** If you are forced to buy a second seat on a connecting or returning flight, don't be rude to the flight attendants. Contact the individual carrier to complain. If you're unsuccessful, contact the Better Business Bureau (BBB) or the Federal Aviation Administration (FAA).

AIRLINE SEATING POLICIES

- AMERICAN AIRLINES — No official policy on buying an extra seat, but if you cannot fit into your seat and need a second one, you have to buy it at full price. Seat belt extenders are available on the plane. Its Web site (*www.aa.com*) has links to seat dimensions.

- CONTINENTAL AIRLINES — All seats in economy class have removable armrests except exit rows and bulkheads. Seat belt extenders are on the plane. If you take up more than one seat, you need to purchase a second one at the current full fare. Flier miles are not available on the second seat.

- DELTA AIRLINES — You do not have to purchase a second seat if you cannot fit into one; however, you must call ahead if you need one. If you need to travel on-peak on a sold-out flight and you purchase a second seat, you will receive frequent flier miles. They do not have an official policy on seat belt extenders.

- JET BLUE — Requests that you purchase a second seat if you feel you need it to fly comfortably. If you cannot buy a second seat, contact Jet Blue and they will try to find you the biggest seat available. Seat belt extenders are available on the plane. Center armrests rise upward.

- NORTHWEST — If you cannot fit into the seat, you have to purchase a second one at the same price. Be sure to notify Northwest as soon as possible that the second seat is for you so that they locate two seats together. Northwest airplanes have moveable armrests, and seat belt extenders are available. Request one from the flight attendant during pre-boarding. If you use an extender, you cannot sit in an emergency row.

- SOUTHWEST — Seat belt extenders are available on the airplane, but you are encouraged to call ahead and ask for them. If you cannot fit in one seat, or if you spill over into the seat next to you, you must purchase a second one at a discounted rate. If the flight is not overbooked, you will be refunded. Southwest asks that if you have purchased another seat for yourself, be sure to tell the flight attendant before you board or when you book. Although Southwest may not seem as bad as other airlines, *Newsday* reported in 2003 that there have been complaints of Southwest forcing people to buy a second seat without any official policy.

- UNITED AIRLINES — Has no official policy for purchasing a second seat, but I was informed that they do not force large-size people to buy more than one seat. Seat belt extenders are available on the airplane.

- USAIRWAYS — They have no official policy regarding necessary extra seating, but if you wish to reserve an additional seat, it must be paid for. Seat belt extensions are available for use on all USAirways flights and may be requested from a flight attendant at the time of boarding.

Buses and trains

- TIME OF DEPARTURE — As with airplanes, it is important to plan your time of departure. Traveling during off-peak hours might allow you to get two seats without problem or incident.

- STANDING — Remember, you're tough. Those stupid skinny people have to sit while you, who are supposed to be the lazy one, proudly stand.

- DON'T BE AFRAID TO TAKE UP MORE THAN ONE SEAT — Remember, the most important thing about self-acceptance is to not allow strangers' glances and comments to ruin your self-esteem. Shoot them a dirty look right back.

- AMTRAK — Coach seats are 19 inches, 6 centimeters and tilt back 35 degrees. If you need to take up a second seat, then you must purchase it. That ticket is refundable if it is not used. Refunds will be subject to whatever penalties are stated with the purchase. If you don't think you'll fit, here's some advice: either buy a second seat and show the ticket to the conductor *only* if he or she asks, then return the ticket, or buy only one ticket before boarding and, if you must, buy a second ticket from the conductor.

- GREYHOUND — On Greyhound seating is first come, first served. You cannot be removed from Greyhound if you are fat. You can be removed if you are drunk, on drugs or breaking the law. Taking up two seats is not breaking the law. However, if you do take up a second seat on a crowded bus, you may be asked to pay a second fare. I recommend following the same guidelines as Amtrak. Middle armrests are sometimes moveable.

Seating in theaters and restaurants

- WHY DRIVE-INS ROCK — Because you sit in your own car and take up as much room as you want! Sadly, there aren't many drive-ins left in the world (ruining the car make-out scene). I recommend the Saco drive-in in Saco, Maine. For $18 a family of four can see *two* currently playing movies. They also have great chili dogs.

- NEW THEATERS VS. OLD THEATERS — Many newer movie theaters have seats in which you can remove the armrests and make two seats into one. Older theaters should be handicap accessible and have a place to put a wheelchair. It is possible to put a chair there if you do not fit in the seat, but be sure to settle this before the show starts. There is no law saying they have to let you sit in the handicap space.

- WHERE SHOULD YOU SIT?
  In live-action theaters — Go for the aisle seat and box seats.
  In restaurants — Go for bench seating or seats without armrests. Check out the restaurant ahead of time to see if you can fit in the seats.

Additional resources

....

AMPLESTUFF: *http://www.amplestuff.com*
Offers a wide variety of items such as large umbrellas, large-size fanny packs, seat belt extenders, large-size garment bags, fitness videos for large people, and medical supplies such as gowns and blood pressure cuffs. The catalog is available online or in print. Phone: (866) 486-1655; fax: (845) 679-1206; e-mail: *amplestuff2@aol.com*

....

SEAT GURU: *http://www.seatguru.com*
Excellent resource for finding seat dimensions on airplanes.

....

NAAFA AIRLINE TIPS FOR LARGE PASSENGERS:
http://www.naafa.org/documents/brochures/airtips.html

"*I am woman, hear me roar, in numbers too big to ignore.*"

HELEN REDDY

CHAPTER 6

FAT CHICKS FIGHT BACK:
Advocacy and Discrimination

During college, I was an active member of the school's feminist group. I devoted countless hours to educating women about serious issues such as rape, sexual harassment and reproductive rights. But something that never came up, even though we were concerned with all kinds of women's issues, was fat acceptance and size discrimination. Despite the fact the so many of the women — both fat and thin — that I worked with and counseled were obsessed with their weight and body image, I never heard the phrase "fat acceptance" until years later. We were the quintessential feminist organization, yet we knew nothing of this battle that affects so many women.

Fortunately, we have come a long away in the decade since I graduated college. All kinds of groups dedicated to fighting fight discrimination have popped up, and the advent of the Internet provides ease in accessing different types of anti-fat-discrimination resources. A movement has formed to help fat chicks fight discrimination and to educate them about their rights and their rightful place in society. As a fat chick, you have an obligation to get involved, and to tell the world about the overlooked plight of the big and beautiful.

There are many ways to be an activist. You should tailor your activism to your interests and personality.

For the shy, simply joining an organization such as NAAFA (National Association to Advance Fat Acceptance) is a big step. Founded in 1969, NAAFA is the big fat grandma of the fat acceptance movement and an organization that is very protest conscious and media savvy. You needn't do more than use your computer, pay a small fee to join, and presto, you can call yourself an activist!

For those who like to put their words down on paper, protest letters are an effective means to register complaints toward specific companies who exhibit anti-fat bias. Make sure to be friendly but firm in your letter, keeping your complaint short, specific and factual. If you are writing to elected officials to complain about a discriminatory law or policy, be sure to mention you are a registered voter. (That will get their attention.) If they are up for reelection, you may want to mention that you think their opponent has an excellent position on this issue. Include your name and address and ask for a reply.

While it's good to write a protest letter, it is as good to write a love letter. What is a love letter? It is writing to a person or organization to compliment them on their pro-fat-acceptance policy. It is good for a business to hear that they are doing something positive. They need to know you got the message and that you support them.

Nine simple things you can do to fight back & increase size acceptance:

1. CREATE A FAT-POSITIVE WEB SITE.

2. WEAR A FAT-POSITIVE BUTTON.

3. SUPPORT MOVIES, TV, BOOKS, ETC., THAT PORTRAY FAT WOMEN IN A POSITIVE LIGHT. REMEMBER, MONEY TALKS!

4. JOIN A FAT ADVOCACY GROUP.

5. IF YOU FEEL LIKE YOU HAVE BEEN DISCRIMINATED AGAINST, FIGHT FOR YOUR RIGHTS. THE MORE CITIES THAT ADOPT LAWS AGAINST SIZE DISCRIMINATION, THE BETTER.

6. REPORT TO THE FEDERAL TRADE COMMISSION ANY DIET PROGRAM MAKING OUTLANDISH CLAIMS. *http://www.ftc.gov*

7. TELL A FAT-POSITIVE JOKE.

8. TRY TO START A PLUS-SIZE EXERCISE PROGRAM AT YOUR JOB OR GYM, OR EVEN START A WALKING GROUP. MANY FAT WOMEN DON'T GET ENOUGH EXERCISE BECAUSE THEY ARE EMBARRASSED.

9. BECOME A RADICAL CHEERLEADER: THE BOD SQUAD — *http://www.lustydevil.com/bodsquad*

Fat advocacy groups

COUNCIL ON SIZE & WEIGHT DISCRIMINATION (CSWD):

http://www.cswd.org

P.O. Box 305, Mount Marion, NY 12456

Phone: (845) 679-1209, Fax: (845) 679-1206

E-mail: info@cswd.org

Formed in 1990 by William Fabrey, the founder of NAAFA, the CSWD is a consumer advocacy group for large people, with a concentration in the area of medical treatment. They run the Medical Advocacy Project, which presents the perspective of the large-size health consumer to the medical and scientific community, and scrutinizes medical research to uncover anti-fat bias.

INTERNATIONAL SIZE ACCEPTANCE ASSOCIATION (ISAA):

http://www.size-acceptance.org

Contact: Allen Steadman

P.O. Box 82126, Austin, TX 78758

E-mail: *director@size-acceptance.org*

Created in 1997, the ISAA's mission is to eliminate size discrimination and increase size acceptance throughout the world. They have many virtual chapters on the Internet and regularly send out activism alerts via e-mail. They also sponsor International Size Acceptance Day.

LARGESSE: THE NETWORK FOR SIZE-ESTEEM:

http://www.eskimo.com/~Elargesse

Created in 1986, Largesse is an online advocacy agency and clearinghouse for fat-positive information. The Web site includes links to International No Diet Day; legal and educational resources; size-positive books, video and print sources; and size-acceptance organizations.

THE NATIONAL ASSOCIATION TO ADVANCE FAT ACCEPTANCE (NAAFA):

http://www.naafa.org

NAAFA, Inc.

P.O. Box 188620 , Sacramento, CA 95818

Phone: (916) 558-6880, Fax: (916) 558-6881

Founded in 1969 by William Fabrey, an average-size man who was upset about how his plus-size wife was treated, the National Association to Advance Fat Acceptance is the big fat grandma of size acceptance groups, with over 5,000 active members. They take a three-pronged approach of advocacy, education and support to fight size discrimination throughout the world. NAAFA members have, among many other forms of activism, participated in demonstrations in protest of Southwest Airlines' discriminatory practices regarding fat passengers and worked to gain legal protection for fat people by serving as a national legal clearinghouse for attorneys challenging size discrimination. They also work to dispel the common myths that are used to justify treating fat people as second-class citizens, extensively using the national media to promote their ideas. Although they are based in Sacramento, they have chapters all over the country and are very active in promoting social groups that support a fat subculture.

....
NATIONAL ORGANIZATION OF LESBIANS OF SIZE (NOLOSE):

http://www.nolose.org

NoLose is a national support organization for large lesbians as well as bisexual and transgendered women. Most of their events occur in the New York area, but there are national activism opportunities, as well as a Web site chock-full of good information.

Work discrimination

A very important issue in the fight against fat discrimination is the workplace. In 1987, NAAFA conducted a survey and found that 62 percent of fat women, 42 percent of fat men and 31 percent of moderately fat women were not hired due to their weight. A 1993 study in the *New England Journal of Medicine* found that fat women earned an average of $6,710 less annually than their thin counterparts. Additionally, there is no nationwide law that protects against weight discrimination, and Michigan is the only state with an anti-weight-discrimination law on the books. According to Susan Carlsen in *A Heavy Problem: Is Obesity a Grounds for Not Hiring?*, you may be able to obtain protection under the Americans with Disability Act of 1990 if you can prove you're disabled because you are obese from an eating disorder and are currently obtaining treatment. You may also be able to sue if you are called a "fat bitch," because that is also gender discrimination.

Like many groups that are discriminated against, fat people, particularly women, have to go beyond what is necessary to prove their worth. So you have to make a decision about whether you want to work harder to prove you are as good as your thin counterparts or take a job in a field that is less competitive, which usually means less pay. But if we keep fighting, discrimination will end. In the meantime, I've included some tips to help you out in the job scene.

- When applying for a job, ensure you are at your very best. All your clothes have to be clean and neat. Wear enough makeup to enhance your beauty, but don't overdo it! Remember, appearances count, and since you are a fat chick, a prospective employer may use your appearance against you, whether he or she is aware of it or not.

- During the interview, be assertive but not pushy, and always make eye contact. Explain your accomplishments and how they will benefit the company. Ask a lot of questions about the company as well. Be sure to thank your interviewer and find out how long it will take before a decision about the position is made. Afterward send a thank-you card.

- If your problem is on the job, keep a file of harassment. Inform your supervisor of any problem. If your supervisor doesn't help, report incidents to your Equal Employment Opportunity Commission Office.

- Be sure to make your superiors aware of your accomplishments. If you feel comfortable with your superiors, you can assure them that your weight has no ill effects on you. If you have not taken a lot of sick time, be sure to point that out.

Legal resources

PERSONS WITH DISABILITY LAW CENTER

http://www.naafa.org/documents/brochures/law_center.html

56 Seventeenth Street N.E.

(Peachtree and Seventeenth)

Atlanta, GA 30309-3245

Phone: (404) 892-4200, Fax: (404) 892-0955

TDD: (404) 892-6027

THE LAW OFFICE OF SONDRA SOLOVAY
AND BEYOND BIAS DIVERSITY TRAINING

http://www.beyondbias.org

2625 Alcatraz Ave., #261

Berkeley, CA 94705

Phone: (510) 839-8743, *sondra@beyondbias.org*

Ms. Solovay is an attorney in private practice who focuses on weight-related discrimination from a civil rights perspective. She also runs Beyond Bias Diversity Training, which provides diversity training for businesses, schools, nonprofits, professionals and conferences. She is the author of *Tipping the Scales of Justice: Fighting Weight-Based Discrimination.*

THE WORKPLACE BULLYING AND TRAUMA INSTITUTE
http://bullyinginstitute.org

U.S. EQUAL EMPLOYMENT OPPORTUNITY COMMISSION OFFICE
http://www.eeoc.gov
1801 L Street N.W.,
Washington, DC 20507
Phone: (202) 663-4900, (800) 669-4000
TTY: (202) 663-4494, (800) 669-6820

"I've been on a diet for two weeks and all I've lost is two weeks."

TOTIE FIELDS

CHAPTER 7

WITTY COMEBACKS AGAINST THE CRUEL & FAT-PHOBIC

One of the worst things that fat people have to deal with is being insulted. Whether it's a nasty comment from some asshole in the street who you accidentally bumped into, or the "best intentions" of family and friends who feel that pointing out your size is somehow helpful (as if you didn't already know yourself), to many, fat people are fair game for insults. So many derogatory terms against fat people — fat bitch, fat pig, fatso, hog, whale, etc. — are part of everyday language that many people use these terms without realizing how hurtful or harmful they can be. Of course, some do use them precisely to be hurtful.

It may be a cliché, but what I have discovered through a lifetime of being the butt of intentional and unintentional fat-phobic comments is that laughter is the best medicine. Instead of flying off the handle at someone who makes fun of you, I find it much better to fight hate or ignorance with intelligence and grace. Using satire and smart humor is the best defense against fat jokes and insults because it helps the unaware to become aware, and shuts the aware up.

I know that in the heat of an insult, it is hard to think of something original and cutting. Well, you don't have to worry anymore — I've come up with some excellent rejoinders to the ignorant and insulting, comments that will make you proud to be a fat person, and make them sorry they ever messed with you.

Roseanne Barr came up with one of the best insults to mean thin people: "I eat the same as you, I just don't puke it up afterward."

In response to:

"FAT BITCH!"
- "Why, thank you!" (*With a big smile*)
- "God loves you, too." (*Substitute Jesus, Allah, Buddha, etc.*)
- Demand a big hug for their kind words.

"YOU LOOK LIKE A WHALE!"
- "Yes, whales are beautiful creatures, aren't they?"
- "Then I would stay away from Seaworld if I were you."
- "Thank you — if you would like to catch my show, call 1-800-23SHAMU."

"YOU HAVE SUCH A PRETTY FACE — IF ONLY YOU'D LOSE WEIGHT."
- "Thank you. It's a shame you have such an ugly face, and you know, I don't think plastic surgery will help. Hope I didn't hurt your feelings."

- "Then I wouldn't have such a pretty face anymore."
- "You have such an ugly soul, and I don't think any amount of weight loss is going to help."

"YOU'VE PUT ON WEIGHT."
- "Thank you."
- "Must be all the great sex."
- "Good, then the diet is working."

"FAT PEOPLE ARE LAZY."
- "You'd be in bed all day too if you had that much sex."
- "I want to work fourteen hours a day, but they will only let me work eight."

"THERE IS A THIN PERSON INSIDE YOU."
- "That's because thin people are so tasty."
- "So, that's what's been kicking me."

"IF YOU EAT LESS, YOU'LL LOSE WEIGHT."
- "Why would I want to do that?" (*Followed by a laugh*)

"HOW COULD YOU GET SO FAT?"
- "By dieting."
- "By eating thin people. Once you pop, you can't stop."
- "I'm actually thin. It's you who is terribly underweight. I know a therapist who can help."

"WOULD YOU LIKE TO TRY OUR DIET PROGRAM?"

- "No."
- "Tried it and gained 20 pounds."
- "No thanks, I'm already on a diet. It's called eating. You should try it."

"YOU COULD LOSE WEIGHT IF YOU WANTED TO."

- "I'd rather have more sex."
- "I'd rather you gain some."
- "Then I wouldn't know where to find it."

"YOU'RE SO FAT AND UGLY."

- "But I still get laid; go figure."
- "You're thin and ugly. Why don't you gain a few pounds and be more like me?"
- "But Jesus still loves me."

"I KNOW A GREAT WAY OF EATING. YOU'LL LOVE IT."

- "Does it involve using your ass instead of your mouth?"
- "I know a great way of eating too. It involves chewing and swallowing."

"YOU NEED TO EXERCISE MORE."

- "After ten orgasms a night, how much more exercise do I need?"
- "Gee, and I thought training for the New York marathon was enough."

"EAT LESS, YOU'LL FEEL BETTER."

- "But I feel better now."
- "Last time I ate less, I ended up in the hospital. But, you know, after all the fainting spells and the constant vomiting, I really did feel better."

"MY FRIEND LOST X POUNDS ON THIS GREAT DIET."

- "Does she still smell?"
- "Is that the diet that causes cancer that I read about in the newspaper?"
- "I did that diet too. Gained 10 pounds."

"YOU DON'T NEED THAT COOKIE."

- "Damn right I do."
- "You're right, I don't need it — I want it."

"OH, THAT [INSERT CELEBRITY] LOOKS SO THIN."

- "I thought she looked dead."
- "Shame she lost her acting ability along with her weight."

"WOULD YOU LIKE TO EXERCISE WITH ME?"

- "No."
- "You couldn't keep up with me, sorry."

"LARD BUTT!"

- "Narrow mind!"
- "At least I have a butt!"

"THAT'S SO FATTENING!"

- "Good."
- "You should eat some, then — you're so skinny."

"CALORIES IN, CALORIES OUT!"

- "Why, that's amazing! Then "Stupid in, stupid out" must work for you."

"300,000 PEOPLE DIE EVERY YEAR OF OBESITY."

- "25,000 die every DAY of starvation."

"IF YOU EXERCISE SO MUCH HOW COME YOU HAVEN'T LOST WEIGHT?"

- "Because muscles are heavy."

"YOU'RE FAT!"

- *(Touch your body and scream.)* "Oh my god!"
- "Really? I never noticed."
- "You're not! What are you waiting for?"

Funny Fat Jokes

"Yo' mama's so fat, when she bungee jumped she went straight to hell."

"How many fat-acceptance zealots does it take to change a lightbulb?"
"I don't know, how many?"
"First, we have to write letters of protest to the company
that made the ladder, because it's only rated for 200 pounds..."

A man was hassling his wife about going on a diet.
"Last time I was at the doctor, he said I had
a good body for my age," she told him.
"And what did he say about your big ass?" he replied.
"Your name never came up."

After getting a checkup, Ralph was told he had a brain tumor and the
only way he could live was if he got a brain transplant. The doctor told
Ralph he could have a thin person's brain for $300,000 and a fat
person's for $150,000.

"Why is the fat person's brain so cheap?" Ralph asked.
"Because it's used."

What do you call a 350-pound stripper?
Rich!

"When we lose twenty pounds... we may be losing the twenty best pounds we have! We may be losing the pounds that contain our genius, our humanity, our love and honesty."

WOODY ALLEN

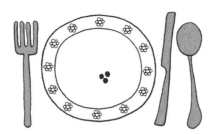

CHAPTER 8

DIETING TO DEATH

One of the dominant themes of our culture today is the celebration of thin and the condemnation of fat. Wherever you look — TV, magazines, books, film — you are hit over the head with the mantra, "You have to be thin so you can be attractive, successful, wealthy," and if you're fat, you better get on your way to being thin. Frances Berg writes in her book *Women Afraid to Eat — Breaking Free in Today's Weight-Obsessed World* that, "At no time in history have women been so pressured to be thin." A study done by Brigham and Women's Hospital in 2000 found that almost all TV commercials aimed at women focused on physical attractiveness.

The messages come fast and furious. Take Miss America, one of the longest running images of beauty in America. A 2000 article in the Journal of the American Medical Association studied the BMI (Body Mass Index) of Miss America pageant winners from 1922 to 1999 and found that the BMI of winners in the 1920s went from an average of 22, which is considered normal, to an average of 18 in the 1990s, considered medically underweight. (And that is with the BMI scam, which I will discuss later in this chapter.) Additionally, a study in the *International Journal of Obesity* found that 70 percent of Playboy centerfolds over the past twenty years were clinically underweight.

Yet, the contrast between what we are and what we are told we should be is astounding. The average American woman is 5'4" and weighs 140 pounds. The average American model is 5'11" and weighs 117 pounds. This means that fashion models are thinner than 98 percent of American women. So, even though the media tells us that an "obesity epidemic" is sweeping the nation, in reality, there is a "thin epidemic" being forced down our throats. The pressure put on people, especially women, to lose weight is enormous. The days of the voluptuous ideal of a Mae West or a Marilyn Monroe are over. To put it succinctly, thin is in, fat is sin. And if we're not thin, we have to lose weight to get with the program.

The "thin" message is loud and clear. A *Cosmopolitan* (what better place to go for contemporary attitudes on body image) survey on body image concluded that:

- 60 percent of women thought they were overweight, where, in reality, 22.6 percent were over the recommended weight range and 24 percent were underweight.

- Only 12 percent were satisfied with their weight.

- 68 percent thought slim women attracted more men and 47 percent thought slim women were happier.

- 72 percent said that they felt models in magazines influenced their body image and 48 percent said women in movies influenced their body image.

On top of all these scary attitudes, adult women are passing the obsession with thinness down to their daughters. A study published in 2003 in the *American Journal of Health Behavior* reported that high school girls tend to see themselves as eleven pounds over their ideal weight, even though they are in fact only three pounds over their ideal weight when computed in BMI. Dr. P. Michael Peterson, who conducted the study, said that "the adolescent infatuation with the cultural icon of thinness has contributed to an array of unhealthy behaviors," adding that such behaviors include poor eating patterns, preoccupation with food and self, extreme dieting, low self-esteem, drug and alcohol abuse, and general physical and mental health problems. Similarly, the article in the *Journal of the American Medical Association* about the incredible shrinking BMIs of beauty pageant winners states that 50 to 75 percent of adolescent girls are dissatisfied with their weight and body image. Like sponges, children are internalizing the messages that thin is right and fat is wrong.

ALMOST HALF OF AMERICAN CHILDREN BETWEEN FIRST AND THIRD GRADES SAY THEY WANT TO BE THINNER.

FOUR OUT OF FIVE TEN-YEAR-OLD CHILDREN ARE AFRAID OF BEING FAT.

HALF OF NINE-AND TEN-YEAR-OLD GIRLS SAY THAT BEING ON A DIET MAKES THEM FEEL BETTER ABOUT THEMSELVES.

The diet epidemic

All of this thinness pressure has erupted into today's dieting epidemic. According to the American Dietetic Association, almost half of the U.S. female population is on a diet at any given time. A 1998 Penn State study placed the figure at 70 percent. The exact figure doesn't matter — most of us have dieted, are dieting, or will be dieting in our lifetime.

This obsession with losing weight has lead to the creation of one of the most lucrative industries in the world today, the diet industry. In America alone, the dieting industry takes in between $40 billion and $100 billion annually. Margo Maine writes in her book *Body Wars: Making Peace with Women's Bodies* that "figures from the late 1990s showed that Americans spent $50 billion annually on diet products... which is the equivalent of the gross national product of Ireland." Diet centers. Group and individual weight loss programs. Prepackaged diet foods. Over-the-counter and prescription drugs. Books and magazines. Physicians, nurses, nutritionists and other professionals specializing in weight loss. Exercise clubs. And on and on. A whole book could be written simply listing the weight loss programs that promise "fast results" or "that you'll be slim by summer." Or fall. Or winter.

But...

And here is the big but from this big butt — dieting doesn't work! Let me say that again for emphasis — DIETING DOESN'T WORK! According to the National Institute of Health, 95 to 98 percent of diets fail within two years, and most people — including yours truly — gain all the weight back and more. John Foreyt, director of the Behavioral Medicine Research Center at the Baylor College of Medicine, has estimated that the average diet lasts only forty-two days, and that only 5 to 10 percent will maintain a significant long-term weight loss.

Dieting is harmful to your health, as it has been linked to a multitude of ailments, both physical and mental. The most well known are eating disorders like bulimia and anorexia. According to a 2004 study published in the *British Medical Journal*, adolescent girls on moderate diets are five times more likely to become anorexic or bulimic than those who do not diet. Those on strict or severe diets are eighteen times more likely to develop an eating disorder. A 2001 article in the *American Journal of Public Health* reported that dieting among adolescent girls — and boys — leads to an increase in smoking initiation.

But that's not the worst of it. According to the Center for Disease Control, there's been an increase in low and very low birth weight babies over the last several decades, which many in the medical community attribute to dieting.

Want more? A large body of research has found that lack of proper nutrition during fetal development activates physiological changes that promote fat formation. In other words, the deprivation patterns of the mother's dieting can help make her baby fat!

Still hungry for more? Teen suicides have tripled over the past forty years, and according to the CDC's Youth Risk Behavior Surveys, teens trying to lose weight or who believe they're overweight are more likely to attempt suicide than those who are happy with their bodies.

In his book *The Obesity Myth*, Paul Campos sums up the harmful effects of dieting: "The efforts of Americans to make themselves thin through dieting and drugs are a major cause of both 'overweight' and the ill health that is wrongly ascribed to it," he writes. He adds that "frequent dieting is perhaps the single best predictor of future weight gain," which supports the evidence that as the battle against the bulge has increased in America over the past several decades, the bulge has actually increased. According to the U.S. Department of Agriculture Center for Nutrition Policy and Promotion, while caloric and fat intake decreased in the United States from 1965 to 1990, obesity increased dramatically. Numerous studies support the claim that the more we diet, the more we weigh.

Yo-yo dieting

Weight cycling (also known as repeat or yo-yo dieting) is when you repeatedly lose and then regain significant amounts of weight. Not only does yo-yo dieting not work, it usually results in significant weight gain — as I can personally attest to. The yo-yo effect can also cause significant health problems. The results of the Framingham Heart Study, a long-term analysis on weight fluctuation, found that people who had a great variety in their weight suffered more heart problems than those who stayed at a stable weight (even if the stable ones were fat). According to findings by researchers at the Fred Hutchinson Cancer Center, yo-yo dieting may have a lasting negative impact on immune function, while maintaining the same weight over time appears to have a positive effect on the immune system. A 2002 study done by the University of Michigan Health Care System concluded that women who went though yo-yo dieting weight cycles, especially five or more times, faced a higher risk of cardiovascular disease after menopause.

Starvation diets

While you may initially lose some weight on a starvation diet, these diets actually slow down the body's metabolism, as it adjusts to the "famine" by expending energy more efficiently to conserve calories. Once a starvation diet is over, people usually gain even more weight back than they lost, making it harder to lose weight the next time. During the diet, one may experience psychological side effects like obsession with food, depression and irritability — and physical effects such as feeling cold. Starvation diets can also lead to binge eating once you return to eating normally. Just ask Oprah!

Eating disorders

Anorexia, bulimia and binge eating disorder (BED) are the most common eating disorders. Anorexia is characterized by self-starvation, which leads to excessive weight loss; binge eating is characterized by periods of uncontrolled eating beyond the point of feeling full; bulimia is binge eating, then forcing yourself to vomit it all up. People with eating disorders use food to compensate for feelings like fear and low self-esteem. Often, an obsession with weight can trigger these life-threatening conditions. A 1997 study in the *International Journal of Eating Disorders* found that 45 percent of binge eaters began doing so after dieting.

My eating disorder of choice, along with many of my fellow fat chicks, has always been binge eating. I remember, one time out of too many, sitting on my kitchen floor and eating an entire cake without enjoying a single bite of it. Afterward, I felt ashamed and disgusted. Often, those who binge do it alone, like an alcoholic who drinks by herself.

Tips to Stop Binge Eating

- LISTEN TO YOUR STOMACH — EAT ONLY WHEN YOU ARE HUNGRY.

- EAT WHAT YOU WANT, WHEN YOU WANT. UNTIL YOU ARE FULL!

- AVOID DIETING!

- DON'T WORRY ABOUT EATING THREE MEALS A DAY — OFTEN FIVE OR SIX SMALL MEALS ARE JUST AS GOOD.

- DON'T BEAT YOURSELF UP WHEN YOU FALL AND BINGE. HUMAN BEINGS ARE NOT PERFECT.

The dieting industry

Like any industry that rakes in the big bucks, the dieting industry needs a lot of repeat business. If diets worked, everyone would only have to use them once, and profits would be limited. So, in order to make money, the dieting industry has to bring you back again and again. And since 95 percent of diets fail, the diet industry is soaring. Taking advantage of our cultural obsession with thinness, the diet industry uses its considerable resources to keep you coming back, even though you are likely to fail each time. You dip into your pocketbook, you buy a product, you lose the weight, you get happy, you gain the weight back with interest, you get depressed, you dip into your pocketbook again, and so on and so on, forever.

And they will stop at nothing to get you to come back, even if they have to lie to do it. A 2002 Federal Trade Commission Report, "Weight-Loss Advertising: An Analysis of Current Trends," reviewed 300 diet ads and found that 55 percent of them made at least one false or unsubstantiated claim. "Lose substantial amounts of weight — including as many as 20 to 40 pounds — without the need to diet or exercise." "Lose weight while you sleep." "Lose 10 pounds and 2 inches in 30 days, without having to change your lifestyle or your eating habits." The diet industry pounds us with information that is at best scientifically unverifiable, and at worst, downright dangerous to our health. And, since the industry is largely unregulated by the government, there is plenty of room for misinformation and misleading information.

Many supposedly neutral and reputable organizations are in cahoots with the dieting industry. The sponsor of both the "Great American Weigh In" and "Shape Up America" is Weight Watchers. The nonprofit group Center for Science in the Public Interest reported that the drug company Wyeth-Ayerst, who created Redux, donated money to the American Dietetic Association and the American Heart Association, among others, to promote their drugs. They also offered grants to the American Diabetes Association, The American Academy of Family Physicians, the North American Association for the Study of Obesity and the American Society of Bariatric Physicians. With an industry that is unregulated, deceptive, and working behind the scenes with supposedly "neutral" organizations, who is there to look out for the fat chick?

Surgery

An NIH report on Gastrointestinal Surgery for the Severely Obese provides a graphic and accurate description of weight loss surgery: "Gastrointestinal surgery for obesity alters the digestive process. The operations promote weight loss by closing off parts of the stomach to... restrict the amount of food the stomach can hold... Some operations combine stomach restriction with a partial bypass of the small intestine. These procedures create a direct connection from the stomach to the lower segment of the small intestine, literally bypassing portions of the digestive tract that absorb calories and nutrients."

The complications from this kind of surgery are harmful, and often deadly. They can include infections, follow-up surgeries to correct complications, or to remove excess skin, gallstones due to significant weight loss in a short amount of time, inflammation of the lining of the stomach, vomiting and anemia. The NIH report goes on to cite that 10 to 20 percent of patients need follow-up surgery, and 30 percent develop nutritional deficiencies. A study presented by Dr. Elmar Merkle at the 2003 annual meeting of the Radiological Society of North American stated that of a study of 335 people who had the operation, 57 had complications within 30 days, 17 patients were readmitted and two died. In addition, numerous studies show that a third of those undergoing surgery gain the weight back.

It used to be that gastric bypass or any weight loss surgery was a treatment only for the severely obese, but nowadays, thanks to the faux-obesity epidemic and the push for thinness, gastric bypass is recommended for people with a BMI of 35 or higher. This means if you are 5'6" and weigh 217 pounds, it is recommended that you get gastric bypass surgery. Even children are undergoing bariatric surgery at a growing rate, even though there are no long-term studies of the effect on this surgery on a person who is still growing.

Dietary supplements

The 1994 Dietary Supplement Health and Education Act (DSHEA) defines a dietary supplement as a product taken orally that adds to a person's diet through the use of nutritional ingredients. Examples of dietary supplements include vitamins, minerals, herbs, and enzymes.

Many fat chicks — including yours truly — have taken these over-the-counter supplements to help us lose weight. However, regulation of diet supplements by the Food and Drug Administration (FDA) is much weaker than regulation for prescription weight loss drugs. While prescription diet drugs must be tested for safety and effectiveness before being put on the market, the FDA views diet supplements as food, which means they do not require approval unless they contain a new ingredient.

Furthermore, the DSHEA places the responsibility of determining whether or not a product is safe on the maker. Before the FDA can recommend that a supplement be taken off the market, it must first proved that it has harmed someone. People have to get sick and maybe die before the FDA can act.

Examples of this backward system are the stories of Ephedra and Fen-Phen. Ephedra, also called Ma Huang, is a naturally occurring substance derived from plants. Ephedra products have been extensively promoted to aid weight loss, enhance sports performance, and increase energy. However, there is little evidence that the herbal supplement actually works and more evidence, as shown by a study that appeared in the March 2003 issue of the *Journal of the American Medical Association*, that it can triple the risk of heart arrhythmias, as well as cause gastrointestinal problems, psychiatric conditions, and dysautonomia. In December 2003, after who knows how much damage was done by this supplement (after the high-profile death of baseball player Steve Bechler, who was taking it to lose weight), the FDA recommended it be taken off the market.

"Fen-Phen" was going to be the miracle appetite suppressive for all us fatties. It consisted of two drugs, fenfluramine and phentermine, which act to alter the serotonin levels in the brain, which can block feelings of hunger. The FDA advised that "Fen-Phen" drugs be removed from the market in 1997 after 79 women and 2 men developed heart valve disease. By the time fen-phen and its cousins were recalled by the FDA, 1.1 million women in the United States were using it to induce weight loss.

Finally, not only is there no evidence that diet supplements help you lose weight, they can actually help you gain weight because of the binge eating that often occurs when the supplement wears off, and rapid weight gain after you go off the supplements entirely.

Support groups for people who want to stop dieting

• NATIONAL CENTER FOR OVERCOMING OVEREATING:

http://www.overcomingovereating.com

Anti-diet support group; workshops, educational material,
centers in several areas, e-mail list

• HUGS INTERNATIONAL:

http://www.hugs.com

A support network for getting off the diet roller coaster;
Hugs Club News, material and workshops for teens

• EATING DISORDER REFERRAL AND INFORMATION CENTER:

http://www.edreferral.com

• ANRED (ANOREXIA NERVOSA AND RELATED EATING DISORDERS):

http://www.anred.com

• NATIONAL EATING DISORDERS ASSOCIATION:

http://www.nationaleatingdisorders.org

"We've been taught to accept this very narrow definition of what is beautiful for women, and we are missing the humanity in people because of what someone may happen to look like."

KATHY BATES

CHAPTER 9

THE WAR AGAINST FAT:

Facts and Misrepresentations

n January 2003, as the United States prepared to invade Iraq, U.S.
Surgeon General Richard Carmona warned that the nation faced a far
more dangerous threat than Saddam Hussein. "Let's look at a threat that
is very real, and already here: obesity." Tommy Thompson, Secretary of
Health and Human Services, has said that "[being] overweight and obesity
are among the most pressing new health challenges we face today."

Thompson and Carmona are just two of a chorus of voices who
have been shouting over the past decade that America is in the middle
of an obesity epidemic, which is not only dangerous to our health —
heart disease, diabetes, you name it — but is also killing us: "Obesity kills
300,000 Americans each year," is the infamous figure I am sure you
are all familiar with. (The number has been recently revised upward to
400,000.)

The words of impending doom are backed by the medical community,
in numerous studies warning of the dangers of being overweight.

Sander L. Gilman, author of *Fat Boys: A Slim Book*, says that "We are in a moral panic about obesity... People are saying, 'Fat is the doom of Western civilization.'" Based on the preponderance of evidence from such reputable sources, there is nothing for us fatties to do except diet immediately, or die eventually.

On the other hand...

What if the government and the medical community and all the other voices screaming about the dangers of being overweight and obese are wrong? (The government and the medical community wrong? Never happened before, has it?) What if, in reality, there is no obesity epidemic, and what if our supposed weight gain isn't killing us, and isn't responsible for our supposedly poor health? What if the medical establishment is distorting the evidence that fat kills? What if fat isn't really the health pariah that everyone would like you to believe it is? What if?

In the last few years, voices have risen against the accepted wisdom that there is a fat epidemic sweeping the nation. These voices come from both those the medical community who believe their fellow practitioners are distorting the "science" of their studies against fat, as well as from activists like Paul Campos and Laura Fraser, who are fighting against the discriminatory practices that the anti-fat hysteria has put into place.

The War Against Fat: In the Beginning

The medical establishment first weighed in on the question of the dangers of fat in 1977, when an NIH conference declared obesity a "disease." Apparently, that declaration wasn't sufficient, so in 1985, the definition was changed to "killer disease." That was followed by the famous 1993 *JAMA* article, which concluded that "300,000 people die each year from illness related to dietary factors and sedentary lifestyle." The "300,000" figure was grabbed by the media, the diet industry and the government as proof that fat kills, and used to launch the war on fat.

In addition to the "300,000" figure, there is also a flood of information that says that being overweight and obese can cause a multitude of chronic and life-threatening diseases and ailments. The NIH lists the following as "Health Risks of Being Overweight."

- Type 2 Diabetes
- Heart Disease and Stroke
- Cancer
- Sleep apnea
- Osteoarthritis
- Gallbladder disease
- Fatty liver disease

The NIH then offers its recommendation on how to avoid the above diseases and ailments. "If you are overweight, losing as little as 5 percent of your body weight may lower your risk for several diseases, including heart disease and diabetes. If you weigh 200 pounds, this means losing 10 pounds. Slow and steady weight loss of 1/2 to 2 pounds per week, and not more than 3 pounds per week, is the safest way to lose weight." In other words, the only way to avoid these catastrophic illnesses, to avoid being one of the "300,000," is by dieting!

Heart disease! Diabetes! 300,000! Get me to Jenny Craig!

Not so fast, my fellow fat chick. Despite the popular sentiment against fat, there are numerous problems with the supposed evidence of health risks from being overweight.

Let's start with the "300,000" figure. Read the exact words from the JAMA article closely. "300,000 die each year from illness related to dietary factors and sedentary lifestyle." The article did not say that "Obesity kills 300,000 each year." This is an important distinction. It was not being overweight or obese that caused the 300,000 deaths, but poor diet — the food we eat — and sedentary lifestyle — i.e., too much time on the couch. Nowhere does the article say that fat kills. The government and the media misrepresented the "300,000" figure to indicate the supposed negative effects of being overweight. As David Levitsky, a nutrition and obesity expert at Cornell University said. "Nobody ever dies of obesity." While obesity may be a marker for other health problems caused by a sedentary lifestyle, it is not dangerous in of itself. Levitsky goes on to say that "if you're a large person and you do not suffer from any other health problems, then there is no reason for you to lose weight."

In addition to the misrepresentation of the "300,000" figure, much of the "science" in the *JAMA* article has come into question. The most damming came in a 1998 *New England Journal of Medicine* article, which stated that "The data linking overweight and death, as well as the data showing the beneficial effects of weight loss, are limited, fragmentary, and often ambiguous... the [300,000] figure is by no means well established. Not only is it derived from weak or incomplete data, but it called into question by the methodologic difficulties of determining which of many factors contribute to premature death."

Risks? What risks?

And what about the actual health risks of being overweight? Take heart disease, for example. According to the American College of Cardiology, "Mortality from heart disease has dropped from 146 per 100,000 people in 1948 to just 87 per 100,000 in 1996." *The New York Times* reported in 2002 that "Dr. Jules Hirsch, an obesity researcher at Rockefeller University provided evidence from studies conducted by others that followed thousands of people for years, keeping track of who lost weight, who kept it off, who become ill and who died. Repeatedly, investigators reported that fat people who lost weight and kept it off had more heart disease and a higher death rate than people whose weight never changed." So, it is not the weight that is causing heart disease, but the effects of dieting.

Diabetes, anyone? In *The Obesity Myth*, Campos quotes Paul Ernsberger, of the Case Western Reserve University School of Medicine, "Actually, there is no hard data that says blood sugar levels are rising." Dr. Ernsberger says that telephone surveys, where many people report themselves as diabetics, are the reasons for the diabetes scare. Additionally, a 2003 article in USA Today found that the CDC was "surprised" to find that diabetes rates have only gone up slightly, from 8.2 percent in 1994 to 8.6 percent in 2000. And this increase, my fat friends, may have been because the definition of Type 2 diabetes was changed in 1997 from a fasting blood sugar of 140 to a blood sugar of 126. As a result of this switch, millions of Americans suddenly became "diabetics."

Sadly, much of the evidence that fat isn't as bad as it is made out to be is suppressed by the media and the medical community. As Frances Berg wrote in a 1998 editorial in *Healthy Weight Journal*, "I have often observed the risks of obesity being exaggerated in academic and federal reports, while eating disorders, dysfunctional eating, nutrient deficiencies, and the hazards of dangerous weight loss treatment are ignored or minimized." Thomas Moore, M.D., of the Boston University School of Medicine, observed that "due to their economic interests and bias, a suppression of research antithetical to the diet industry's position exists. Research not supporting weight loss isn't funded and isn't published."

The powers that be are so convinced that there is fat is killing us that they are willing to overlook the flaws of the very science that they base their conclusions on. As Paul Campos says, "the war on fat has reached the point where the systematic distortion of the evidence has become the norm, rather than the exception."

Fortunately, activists like Campos are helping to bring the view that fat doesn't kill to a wider audience. And maybe, just maybe, the medical community is starting to see the light. A study published in 2002 in the *Annals of Epidemiology* showed that the best predictor of ill health is being inactive, regardless of weight. The study concluded that small amounts of physical activity were "significantly protective." The lead author of the study, Carlos J. Crespo, Dr.P.H., associate professor of social and preventive medicine in the University at Buffalo's School of Medicine and Biomedical Sciences said that "Consistently, physical inactivity was a better predictor of all-cause mortality than being overweight or obese." Furthermore, the study found that *underweight* people were at greater risk of dying from any cause than people of healthy weight. In the next chapter, I will discuss how important it is to be a fit fat chick!

The great BMI hoax: Thin today, fat tomorrow

BMI (Body Mass Index) is the measurement of fat content in your body. It is determined by dividing your weight in kilograms by your height in meters squared. In other words, it uses your weight and height to come up with a number. Simple, right? No so simple.

When I was trolling around looking for a "scientific" definition of BMI, I came upon the following on the NIH Web site, "Body mass index (BMI) is a method that can be used to estimate whether you are a healthy weight. Being overweight puts strain on your heart and can lead to serious health problems. These problems include type 2 diabetes, heart disease, high blood pressure, sleep apnea, varicose veins, and other chronic conditions. More than 300,000 lives could be saved in the U.S. each year if everyone maintained a healthy weight!" Instead of offering a scientific definition, the NIH offers an opinionated definition of BMI. Instead of offering science, the NIH offers judgements!

Furthermore, the definition of overweight as calculated by BMI can be changed at the government's whim. In 1998 the definition of "overweight" was changed from anyone having a BMI (Body Mass Index) over 27, (which for a American woman of average height, 5' 4", is 157 pounds) to anyone with a BMI over 25 (which for the 5'4" woman is 145 pounds). Without gaining a pound, 29 million Americans became overweight, at risk from the "killer disease" of fat, and, of course, targets from the diet industry.

To give you some examples of what BMI means in the real world, actor Bruce Willis, at 6 feet and 211 pounds has a BMI of 29. Tom Cruise, at 5 feet 7 inches and 201 pounds, has a BMI of 31. Sylvester Stallone, 5 feet 9 inches and 228 pounds, has a BMI of 34. California governor Arnold Schwarzenegger, at 6 feet 2 inches and 257 pounds, has a BMI of 33. All overweight. All unhealthy? I think not.

There is a great controversy viewing over the true effects of BMI on your health. Paul Campos has stated that most of the studies used to calculate the relationship between BMI and health risks show that those deemed "overweight" in fact have lower death rates than those who are underweight. As he points out, "the BMI cannot factor in the vast variations in body makeup... Some people have more muscle or more bone density, making the index misleading."

Dr. Peter Katzmarzyk, a spokesperson for the Heart and Stroke Foundation of Canada, believes that fitness levels and smoking are the most important factors in determining health, not weight and BMI.

Margaret MacNeill, director of the Centre for Girls' and Women's Health and Physical Activity Research at the University of Toronto says that" The BMI is a number (on a scale), not a fact... However, the index is being used by doctors, dietitians and some educators to set weight goals for individuals, a practice that is dead wrong." She goes on to say that the BMI index "'tyrannizes' people, especially women, who are conditioned to strive for unrealistic and unhealthy weights."

Why are we fat? It's the genes, stupid!

Despite myths to the contrary, studies show that we fat people eat about the same amount as thin people. Then, you may ask, why aren't all fat people thin, or conversely, all thin people fat? The reason may be in our genes — because fat people have a higher "set-point" than thin people.

The term "set-point" was made popular by William Bennett and Joel Gurin in their book *The Dieter's Dilemma*. The idea of a set point is that your body is genetically determined to weigh within a certain rate — be it thin, medium or fat — and that there is nothing you can do about it.

The science behind the theory is that your body keeps track of it's fat stores or reserves, increasing or decreasing the burning of fat and calories, your metabolism, in order to maintain a consistent level of fat. As the body monitors its fat storage, it produces hunger or fullness by releasing or suppressing the amount of leptin, a hormone released by fat cells, in order to keep those stores constant at your set-point.

As more fat is stored in the cells, your leptin levels rise, which signals the hypothalamus to suppress appetite. Falling levels do the opposite, stimulating appetite. So, when you are on a diet, your leptin levels fall, making you hungry.

Fat people have a higher set point at which their leptin levels are triggered. This means that when we try to lose weight, the amount of calories we consume at rest, which is called the basal metabolic rate, decreases to counteract all of our weight loss efforts. (However, the higher leptin levels make also make us enjoy sex — more on that later.)

Everyone has different set-points. You could be the same height as someone, yet their set-points could be twenty — or one hundred — pounds less, or more. And, there is no test to tell you what your body's natural set point is. The best way to determine it is by eating normally and exercising moderately. If you have been dieting for a long time, it can take up to a year of normal eating for your body's metabolism to function properly again, and return to your natural set-point.

The thrifty gene

The thrifty gene hypothesis, developed by geneticist James Neel, goes back to early humans civilization, when feast-or-famine conditions reigned. In order to get us through the times when there wasn't enough food, the "Thrifty Gene," developed, which would help you to hold on to your fat in the long gap between meals. This gene was helpful as long as there were periods of famine. But once we adopted our modern standard of living and eating — a high fat diet, with less physical activity — the gene began to work against us, storing calories in preparation for a famine that will never come.

"Lack of activity destroys the good condition of every human being, while movement and methodical physical exercise save it and preserve it."

PLATO

CHAPTER 10

FAT & FIT ARE JUST FINE!

The Cooper Institute for Aerobics Research in Dallas studied the fitness habits of 25,000 middle-aged men and 8,000 women over a ten-year period. Fitness levels were measured by how long people could walk on a treadmill at increasing intensity before becoming exhausted. The results indicated that it's better to be fit and fat than thin and sedentary, and that exercise, regardless of weight, is the key to health and a long life.

"There's too much focus on BMI and body weight," says Steven Blair, president and CEO of the Cooper Institute. He says that most studies on the dangers of obesity have not adequately accounted for the impact of exercise. "There is a misdirected obsession with weight and weight loss... The focus is all wrong. It's fitness that is the key." Blair said 30 minutes of moderate walking every day, at three or four mph, would make most obese people fit.

He also said that obese people who exercise have half the death rate of those who are trim but don't exercise. "I don't mean it eliminates the risk of everything, but you can stay overweight and obese if you are fit and be just as healthy, in terms of mortality risk, as a lean fit person." John E. Blundell, chair of psychobiology at the University of Leeds in England, agreed with Blair. "I'm inclined to agree with that. I don't think that carrying around a lot of fat, in itself, is necessarily detrimental because a number of large people are very vigorous."

In addition, the Cooper study also looked at diseases supposedly connected to being overweight, particularly diabetes. "The phenomenon holds there too that the obese individuals who are fit develop diabetes at about the same rate as the lean individuals who are unfit," Blair concluded.

So, the evidence is in — fat and fit is the way to go, thin and lazy is the way to die. Even moderate exercise three times a week will decrease your health risks for heart disease, diabetes and cancer. It will also help with back problems, and lower cholesterol. Exercise will also increase your self-esteem, as it releases endorphins, which make you feel damn good!

The most important thing about exercise is do it for enjoyment and not for weight loss. I've compiled a list of fun ways to get physical.

• WALKING — You should try walking twenty minutes to an hour per day. It is a good way to get rid of stress and to learn to appreciate what is around you. When you walk study the world. Learn what makes it beautiful. For those of you in colder climates, mall walking is a good way to go. You can count how many clothing stores that cater to small sizes are going out of business.

• SWIMMING — Swimming is my favorite sport and "looking bad" in a bathing suit has never stopped me from doing it. Be daring, don't wear a t-shirt over your bathing suit or wear a bikini.

- YOGA — Yoga is an exercise that EVERYONE should be doing. It keeps your body flexible, your mind free from stress and your spirit soaring. Not all yoga instructors understand that there are positions that can make fat women uncomfortable, so be sure to find an instructor who is sensitive to this issue.

- DANCING — Show 'em that fat people have all the moves!

- TRAIL/HIKING — One of my most pleasant memories was hiking up a mountain in New Mexico. It was a difficult climb, but it was well worth the view at the end. Every state has trails or hiking. Even cities do. Go at your own pace.

- BIKING — Biking decreases the chance of cardiovascular disease. Biking instead of driving decreases congestion and pollution. Be sure to wear a helmet.

- LOW IMPACT WEIGHT LIFTING — To be fat and muscular

- SKIPPING — Most people will get out of the way of a 300-pound woman skipping down the street.

- PROTEST MARCHES/BENEFIT WALKS — To be physically and socially active

- MARTIAL ARTS — Then you can carry a wood board with you and if someone makes fun of your weight, you can break the board in front of them.

- SEX — Go insane.

Exercise resources

REAL FITNESS FOR REAL WOMEN. This book by Rochelle Rice creates an easy to follow fitness plan for large women that requires very little equipment and no gym memberships.

GREAT SHAPE: THE FIRST FITNESS GUIDE FOR LARGE WOMEN. This book by Pat Lyons and Debby Burgard shows exercises made for larger bodies.

KELLY BLISS OFFERS FITNESS FOR LARGE WOMEN. She also puts out fitness tapes. *http://www.kellybliss.com*

NAAFA AND ISAA are good resources to try to find exercise programs for plus sizes in your area or you can start your own. *http://www.infitnessinhealth.com*

Healthy eating

I don't want to lecture you on eating. You've been lectured your whole life on proper nutrition by family, friends, physicians, strangers, and talk show hosts. I want to address eating because I think a lot of fat chicks, particularly chronic dieters, have a convoluted idea of healthy foods.

Let's take a look of some of the things I once thought were healthy: ice milk, Dexitrim, frozen dinners, diet cookies, fat free muffins, high sugar diet shakes and low carbohydrate highly processed candy bars. As you can see, I didn't make great food choices. When I stopped dieting, I didn't have a clue what to eat. Should I eat a lot of carbs? Is butter OK?

How about red meat? Should I be a vegetarian? Should I get my fat from olive oil or peanut butter? Should I have a glass of wine? Orange juice? What about food allergies? Should I eat when my stomach growls or when I feel hungry?

It is important that all chicks, fat and skinny, eat as well as they can. This means using common sense. Eat things that are good for you, like fruits and vegetables. Eat fish, eat meat, eat chicken. Have some bread. Don't abandon foods that you enjoy that may be "bad" for you, like sweets. They should be a part of what you eat, too. You don't want to force yourself to avoid certain foods — that will lead to bingeing. By using common sense, you will learn to eat a balance of proper foods, while at the same time still enjoying your treats.

It is also very important to eat normally. Normal eating is eating at regular times, when you are hungry, whether it be the traditional three meals a day, or more frequent, smaller meals. Dysfunctional eating consists of irregular (skipping meals) or chaotic eating (fasting, bingeing, dieting).

You should only eat when you are hungry — and then stop when you are satisfied. Some days you will eat more, some days less, but on the whole, you should eat the same everyday. One of the key ways to know the difference between normal and dysfunctional eating is that after eating normally you should feel pleasantly full, and after dysfunctional eating, like a binge, you will feel bad, both physically and emotionally.

"The New England Journal of Medicine reports that nine out of ten doctors agree that one out of ten doctors is an idiot."

JAY LENO

CHAPTER 11

THE DOCTOR WILL SEE YOU NOW:

Dealing with the Medical Profession

ost women reading this book are probably familiar with the "lecture." You know, the one your doctor gives you, whether you want it or not. I'm talking, of course, about the fat lecture, the one where the doctor sits you down, and in his — usually *his* — most authoritarian voice, tells you that you have to lose weight. After this talking to, your feel ashamed and angry. I've been lectured on my weight at least five times by doctors, twice by the same one.

In addition, many doctors treat fat people and thin people differently when it comes to medical care. In *Tipping the Scales of Justice*, author Sondra Solovay says that a survey of over 1,300 doctors found 17 percent of them didn't want to do a pelvic exam on a fat woman, while none had a problem doing it for thin women. She also related an example of when a picture of a thin woman was presented to 120 members of the American

Psychological Association, and later, the photo was altered to make the woman look fat. While "both" women were presented with the same case history, the second woman was diagnosed with more psychological problems than the first.

Choosing a doctor

Always remember that it is you who hired the doctor, so he or she needs to earn your respect, not the other way around. It's important that all women, fat and thin, go to the doctor, dentist, and gynecologist at least once a year.

If you are looking for a health professional who is fat-friendly, you may find one at: *http://www.cat-and-dragon.com/stef/fat/ffp.html*

YOU SHOULD RUN SCREAMING FROM YOUR DOCTOR'S OFFICE IF:

1. The doctor gets angry when you refuse to be weighed or won't look at the scale or discuss the number. However, there are times when being weighed is necessary. Once, when I told one of my many doctors I didn't want to be weighed, he said it was important to do it to figure out the dosage of medication. The only other time weight should be of concern is if you gain or lose it rapidly for no reason.

2. If you get this kind of message on your answering machine. "I have the results of your blood test, everything is normal. Stay on your diet." When I got that message on my machine, I changed doctors. If your tests are normal, then you shouldn't worry.

3. Your doctor makes fun of your weight.

4. You go in to be treated for the flu and your doctor blames it on your weight.

5. Your doctor keeps trying to send you to this nutritionist friend of his who knows about this great diet.

6. Your doctor tells you to get surgery for your weight. No doctor should advocate surgery except for an emergency.

7. Your doctor tries to push diet products on you.

8. Your doctor says the reason he can't find a vein to draw some blood is because of your weight.

9. You've had healthy blood tests since the dawn of time and you eat right and feel good. Despite that, the doctor still calls you a ticking time bomb.

Your rights at the doctor's office

If you feel any of these rights have been broken, change doctors. NAAFA has a good document on the rights of fat people with seeking medical treatment. I've adopted some of their suggestions and added a few of my own:

1. You have the right not to be weighed or not to look at the number (and the right to refuse treatment).

2. You have the right not to be ridiculed. Your doctor should be friendly and looking out for your best interest.

3. You have the right to decide what is best for your health.

4. You have the right to a second opinion. If the doctor won't give you a referral, find a doctor who will.

5. You have the right to change doctors.

6. You have the right to be treated with dignity

7. You have a right not to be discriminated against.

8. You have a right to privacy.

....

9. You have a right to the same health care as other patients.

....

10. You have the right to the best care available.

Questions to ask while trying to find a fat-friendly doctor

It is always important before you get a new doctor that you contact them and ask them a few questions about their opinions on fat. If they seem hesitant or unwilling to answer our questions, it is probably not a good idea to use them. You can also write them a letter if you feel uncomfortable talking to them on the phone.

....

1. Do you consider weighing mandatory? Don't hang up the phone if they say yes. The doctor may need your weight to prescribe the correct dosage of medication.

....

2. What do think about fat individuals? You may not get an honest answer, but you should ask.

....

3. Are you attached to any weight loss program? If yes, hang up. Your doctor should be free of any kind of commercial affiliations.

....

4. Does the office have comfortable seating? Are the seats big enough to accommodate you?

5. Do you think a person can be fit and fat? This is very important. Your doctor should be helping you get fit, not lose weight.

6. Are you uncomfortable with touching a fat person? Some doctors are so fat phobic they are afraid to touch you. You may not get an honest answer, but you should ask. Sometimes you can hear the answer from the tone of voice.

7. Do they know about the 95 percent dieting failure statistic? If they don't, you can educate them.

8. What do they think causes obesity? If they say discipline, run screaming!

9. Do they own equipment that can accommodate your size? (If they don't have big gowns, buy your own. It's easier. You can write it off as a medical expense.)

10. Do they offer nutritional counseling without pushing weight loss?

Questions to ask a psychologist/psychiatrist

1. Do they think a fat person can be happy psychologically?

2. Do they understand the issues that fat women have to deal with?

3. Will they have problems dealing with me accepting my weight?

4. Can they deal with your eating disorder without pushing dieting?

Be aggressive and responsible

Remember this is *your* health. You have a right to know about it. You have a right to discuss it. Don't always believe what the doctors says if it sounds uncomfortable. For example if you need an operation but your doctor won't do it unless you lose weight. Find another d

"If we did all the things
we are capable of,
we would literally
astound ourselves."

THOMAS EDISON

CHAPTER 12

FEELING GROOVY:
Developing Positive Self-Esteem and Self-Worth

We live in an instant-gratification society, but change is not something that happens in an instant. It takes time and patience to undo bad habits, and there is no magic pill, not even lithium, that can help you gain self-esteem. You have to work on it. You have spent a lifetime being putdown and having your self-esteem denigrated, so you shouldn't expect things to change overnight.

However, whether you realize it or not, as a fat chick in a thin-centric world, you already are more courageous than most. You have lived with being ostracized, ridiculed and rejected. But, you know something? You're still here, and if you are reading this book and books like this, then you have taken the first steps to healthy self-esteem. And, if you are willing to continue embracing yourself as a fat chick, one day you will become a fat chick who rules! Then, there is nothing you can't do.

Don't despair if doesn't all come at once — it doesn't. You will have good days and bad days, fallbacks and revelations, on your way to healthy self-esteem. You are not perfect. It is OK to take baby steps. It is OK to fail, as long as you try again. As Frederick Douglass said, "If there is no struggle, there is no progress." Realize that the road to self-esteem has several steps: self-respect, confidence and courage. As time goes on, you will feel better and better, and then each day will be more spectacular than the next, and you will look forward to your fat future with energy and optimism.

In order to help you down the road, here are some suggestions that worked for me on my road to fat acceptance and self-esteem. Each one of you has to tailor your path to your own needs, desires and personality. However, I hope that my suggestions can at least give you some ideas.

Accept the fact you aren't going to be thin

While you say you accept your size, I know that many of you still secretly wish a magic pill will come along and make you a perfect size 6. I used to tell people that I accepted who I was, when deep down I really hadn't. Accepting your weight is one of the hardest things for fat chicks to do. Every day, we are bombarded with images that make us feel bad about ourselves. It is OK to have doubt — you probably always will on some level. However, if repeat to yourself the following mantra when things get tough, *I am fat, I am beautiful*, you will start to have more and more days where you don't feel bad about your body. Eventually, you will actually feel good about your body all the time. And, then you will start to...

Love your body

Every morning, take off all your clothes and look into the mirror and tell yourself you're beautiful. Look at every part of your body and tell that part that you love it, especially to the parts of the body you used to be ashamed of. Don't be afraid to touch the parts of the body you used to hate. Always view your body with love and try to stop hate talk before it starts. In *When Women Stop Hating their Bodies*, Jane Hirschmann and Carol Munter recommend that if you say bad things to your body, immediately apologize to your body and challenge the hate talk. You must learn to love your body so that your happiness doesn't depend on the scale.

Master body language

Body language tells a lot about you. The way you sit and stand, use your eyes, and hands, lets the world know exactly how you feel without you even uttering a word. A couple of useful tips on body English:

- Don't cross your arms in front of your stomach. Most people may prefer reality shows over reading, but they are smart enough to know that you are fat even if you cover your stomach. Don't be afraid to show your body.

- Looking at the floor means you are subservient; looking at the sky means you are a dreamer. People will respect you more if you maintain eye contact. It shows that you are assertive.

- When you are in a social gathering, stand straight and tall. Don't lean against the wall as if your weight is threatening to drag you to the ground at any moment.

- Sit more than you stand. You don't want to be stereotyped as the fat girl in the corner.

- Don't let the party come to you. Get actively involved in conversations. The more people get to know your wonderful personality, the more they will see you as a person.

Use humor

It is important, whether you are thin or fat, to keep a sense of humor. It can help you against the ignorant and fat-phobic, and it can keep you from internalizing negative emotions. Remember, laughter helps you to live longer. When you are talking to someone and they make a fat joke, don't automatically reject them. You know the difference between harmless fun and an outright insult. You don't want to be a doormat, but you can lighten up. Sometimes, the most politically incorrect people can also be the most honest. I would rather have someone acknowledge my weight with a friendly joke, then have someone be nice to face, and criticize me behind my back later. And, even if someone is mean and insulting to your face, it is better to laugh it off — and then not talk to that person again! Rising above is more beneficial than being hurt.

Control your fear

Don't ever be afraid to take up space. Fat people often become afraid of trying new things because, unlike their thin counterparts, they are some times ridiculed when they do things expected only of "thin" people. This causes them to be shy and fearful in work and relationships. Conquering fear is a hard thing. I suggest that once a day you do something that you are afraid of. It could be something simple like dealing with a difficult person, or more difficult, like asking for a raise or a date. Take small steps toward assertiveness and do not revert back into a wallflower when you receive rejection. Remember, no matter what your size, life is full of rejection. You must get past that, and embrace the positive, and defeat the fear that would hold you back.

Appreciate your accomplishments

Every morning after you prance around naked, tell yourself everything you have done. If you don't feel like you have accomplished anything, go out and try something new.

Get over the past

As hard as it may be, leave the past in the past. For those of you are who still in high school or younger, a word of wisdom — once you are an adult, no one will know whether you were a prom queen, geek or football player. No one will care that you dated the football hero, threw up in the cafeteria, or once came to school with your shirt inside out. Hurtful things from the past can have a powerful negative affect on self-esteem, so you need to let those things go. In the end, you are the only person you are hurting.

In my early 20s, through therapy, I revisited my past and decided to forgive all the people who had teased me over the years (and there were a lot, trust me, including some of my own family). Now, I no longer look upon of that part of my life with resentment or bitterness. Forgiveness will free you from the past.

Doing things you wouldn't ordinarily do — Take some risks!

A lack of self-esteem results in fat chicks often not doing fun and challenging things. Once you have conquered your fear — or at least have it under control — make a list of things you planned to do when you got thin — and do them *now*. Life without risk is called death. Here are some things you could try:

- You're not going to get thin! So, go through your closet and toss anything that doesn't fit and won't ever fit. A good rule of thumb is that if you haven't worn it in two years, you're not going to wear it in two hundred years. Once you have tossed out your old clothes, go to Torrid, Lane Bryant, Talbots Woman, Goodwill, whatever, and buy a chic new wardrobe.`

- If you have the money, go on a super vacation to someplace you would have never gone before. If you're broke, go camping or on a long drive, or take a long train ride.

- Wear clothes that fat people shouldn't wear. Wear a belly button shirt even if your fat sticks out.

- Volunteer — not just in the size acceptance movement, but any kind of movement, Pro-life, pro-choice, Nature, Loggers, War, Peace, Vegan, Carnivores, Radical Nazi Dentists, the Moral Majority. Whatever the issue don't be afraid to take the reins.

- Support the Fat Arts. Surrounding yourself with books, movies and artwork that reveal positive fat images will make you feel better and change your ideas on what is beautiful.

If you have done some or all of the above and feel ready for something more challenging, here are some suggestions that will really put you out there. Remember, don't take these kind of steps until you feel absolutely ready.

Become a size-acceptance advocate

It is very important to fight for size acceptance. If you don't have a lot of time, you can write a letter a week against an "anti-fat" business. If you have the time, volunteer at your local NAAFA or ISAA chapter. If there isn't one near you, form your own. Helping other people accept their size will make you feel good about your own size.

Become a plus-size model

If you think you can hack it, plus-size modeling can greatly enhance self-esteem. If you go through an agency, be sure they are reputable and do not charge you (agencies should make commissions off your jobs). If you decide to go freelance, create a portfolio of different poses, as well as a composite sheet with your best pictures. Unfortunately, the look for plus-size models seems to be size 12, tall and toned, but there are some places that need bigger models.

Resources

....

BIG, BOLD, BEAUTIFUL WOMEN:

http://www.bbbwomen.com

....

PLUS SIZE ACADEMY:

http://www.theplusacademy.com

....

PLUS SIZE WOMAN CONVENTION & PAGEANT:

http://www.plususa.com

Dimensions Plus, Canton, OH

(330) 649-9809, Fax (330) 649-9309

E-mail: *info@plususa.com*

RESOURCES TO HELP YOUR SELF-ESTEEM

....

Hutchinson, Marcia Germaine. 200 WAYS TO LOVE THE BODY YOU HAVE

....

LIVING LARGE SERIES by Cheri K. Erdman.

Two books that give you affirmations to learn to love yourself
and your large body.

....

NATIONAL ASSOCIATION FOR SELF-ESTEEM:

http://www.self-esteem-nase.org

....

SELF-ESTEEM LEARNING FOUNDATION: *http://www.selfesteem.org*

"I'm sorry, but Madonna has nothing on me as a rebel. Madonna in a thong, me in a thong — which one is more challenging to the status quo?"

MARILYN WANN

CHAPTER 13

YOU ARE SO BEAUTIFUL:
Tips for Looking Hot

I know that many of you wake up in the morning, take one look in the mirror, and decide that, as a fat woman, there is no point in putting on makeup or doing your hair. Well, when you *were* a fat woman, maybe that kind of thinking was OK. But now you are a fat *chick*, and you rule! You're beautiful, bodacious and bountiful, and that means using every means at your disposal, both natural and artificial, to look your hottest.

I get fed up seeing so many of my sisters walking around in frumpy clothes, bad haircuts and no makeup, saying, "it doesn't matter how I look, I'm fat." Hiding your curvaceous assets underneath shapeless clothing, and striving for a non-sexual, non-attention getting appearance projects low self-esteem, and is a no-no.

And don't give me the answer, "when I lose x pounds, I'll start working on looking beautiful." That is just an excuse, and besides, we all know that dieting doesn't work. Stop planning for a day you're going to buy size 6 dresses, designer couture and Seven Jeans. You're beauty starts *today!* Do you want to spend years hiding in a locked box, waiting for your magical thin day, instead of getting out there and living a fabulous life? Take your clues from celebrities such as Monique and Camryn Manheim. They dress to the nines, show off their cleavage and look absolutely fabulous. And you can too!

Here are some suggestions for becoming the best-looking fat chick on your block:

Clothing

- Do you want to buy that fabulous gold tank top, but think you should wait until you're smaller? Stop that thinking. Buy it in your current size and wear it now!

- Bigger clothing does not hide your figure. Bigger is not better, it just makes you look frumpy. Wear clothing that cuts close to your silhouette and emphasizes your figure. Proportion is the key. Wear fitted pieces on parts you wish to emphasize. Ladies, show off that booty! Who can forget Sir Mix-A-Lot's homage, "Baby Got Back"?

- If you want to play up your bust, look for a shirt that has a horizontal stripe that crosses the front. Vertical stripes lengthen the body and will bring out the length of your legs.

- Always look for stretch clothing. They offer smooth lines and are extremely comfortable.

- Do not be afraid to put on a pair of high heels and a short skirt. Heels are meant to show off your legs. Think sexy style, not no-style.

- Accessories, accessories, accessories. A funky pair of glasses, a fun handbag, a colorful scarf can liven up any outfit and create an attention-getting look. Exquisite shoes and a beautiful bag are the keys to looking chic, no matter what size you are.

Makeup

- You are beautiful, so put on some lipstick and flex those lips!

- Add a touch of eye shadow to bring out your eyes.

- A quick dusting of shimmering powder over the high points of the face can do wonders.

- Choose light shades and start with only one or two products. As you gain confidence, move up to more complex items.

- Don't be afraid to experiment.

- If you have absolutely no knowledge of makeup, see a professional or pick up Sonia Kashuk's Real Beauty, an essential for any fat chick doing a makeup overhaul.

A few makeup "don'ts":

- Avoid wearing too much. Makeup is meant to enhance features, not bring negative attention. (How many times have you noticed bad makeup jobs on other women?) When you're done, your makeup should look natural.

- Thick eyeliner will give you raccoon eyes and make you look overdone. Too much mascara will turn you into Tammy Faye Baker.

- Make sure your foundation is the same color as your skin, and blend it well. Don't pour it on, dot it on and then blend, blend, blend, so your neck is not a different color from your jaw line.

- Go easy on the powder — not too much, and again, blend it well.

Go to the spa!

Every fat chick needs to spend a day at the spa. No, not one of those crazy spas where you check in for a week of dieting and purging. I'm talking about a day spa, where you can ditch the stress and indulge in facials, massages, aromatherapy, reflexology and waxing. You deserve to be pampered. We get exhausted trying to ignore anti-fat messages and junk science. Its time for fat chicks to spend a day at the spa!

And while you're there... get your nails done. There's nothing like red-hot nails that scream, "I'm gorgeous!"

Hair

Bad haircuts continue the "I'm fat, therefore I'm ugly" myth. Get a stylish cut that emphasizes your gorgeous cheekbones and don't be afraid to use a little color. Color is all the rage and a skilled colorist can add wonderful depth to your face.

Celebs say, "It's all about the skin!"

Emme's secret to beauty is "good genetics! And the other thing to keep the genetics going is cleansing my face every single night, followed by moisturizer, 16 ounces of water, and at least six to seven hours a week of sleep." Star Jones reportedly uses baby wipes to moisturize and Mo'Nique drinks lots of water, cleanses her face with astringent and uses a moisturizer.

Beauty on a dime

Don't want to use beauty products that have been tested on animals or participate in the corporate beauty markup? Feeling cheap? Don't have money to spend on buying a whole new beauty regimen? Then use your refrigerator to make homemade products. Honey works well to tighten the pores and moisturize the skin. Use it directly on your face, coating your skin. Leave it on until it dries, and then rinse it off. Or make a moisturizer from olive oil, adding lavender and sandalwood for scent.

Some more issues for fat chicks

SWEAT. Fat chicks are hot hot hot! So we tend to sweat more more more. Corn starch (it's cheaper and less problematic than talc) will help keep things dry. Vagisel powder is recommended for the crotch area, as well as between your thighs and under your boobs. Put some in your bra too. Also, apply deodorant more than once a day. Tired of trashing your light-colored shirts because they are permanently stained? Buy sweat-guards to wear underneath your clothes.

CHAFFING. Bicycle shorts under your skirt will stop chaffing. Modells carries them in sizes up to 4x.

"We control 50 percent of a relationship. We influence one hundred percent of it."

ANONYMOUS

CHAPTER 14

NO MORE SITTING AT HOME ON SATURDAY NIGHT:
Dating and Romance

One of the most important, if not the most important, issues that affect fat chicks, like all other chicks, are relationships. Despite what the media and some people might tell you, we all know that fat people have the same needs and desires as the rest of the world. Most of us want to date, maybe meet that special somebody. Most of us also want to get laid from time to time.

Being overweight makes dating and sex hard for many fat chicks. Since we have been told throughout our lives — by both the outside world and our own inner voices — that we are unattractive, ugly and undesirable, it is difficult for a lot of fat women to feel comfortable in the dating world. A 2002 article in *Obesity Research* found that "obese girls were less likely to date than their peers," and that "both obese boys and girls reported being more dissatisfied with their dating status compared with average-weight peers." Many of us — including, for many years, this fat chick — retreat into isolation, and shy away from social settings in order to repress our feelings of shame. Dating is hard enough without the added stigma of weight dragging you down.

Other women, feeling that they are lucky to find anyone who is interested in them, get into unhappy or abusive relationships. A 1995 study, published in the *Journal of Family Issues*, concluded that obese women were happier with their marriages because they recognized "their decreased value in the marriage market in a society that stigmatizes obesity." "In other words, women appear to internalize and accept the negative assessments of their obesity," the article said.

Don't date until you're ready

To meet someone else, you have to first feel good about yourself. In the chapter on self-esteem, I discuss several ways for you to feel better about you are, and realize that you are fat and beautiful, not just fat. Following those tips will improve your self-confidence, and only when you have adequate self-confidence can you feel comfortable approaching another person. My biggest piece of advice is don't push it. Even if all your friends are dating, getting married, etc., you should not enter the dating game until you are good and ready. Remember — it's your life, and no one else's, and you should do things when you are ready.

But if you are ready...

Try some of the beauty tips suggested in the previous chapter. It will make you feel good to look good. As for the rest, you should recall one simply word — settling! When I talk about settling, I mean dating with someone who doesn't treat you like an equal. Someone who thinks you're so desperate for a relationship that they can treat you like dirt. Be careful of them, because they do exist. (There is a practice called "hogging" in which men search out fat women for easy sex.) As a fat chick, you should not feel that you should have to settle for the bottom of the barrel.

Some handy-dandy advice about socializing and dating

- Don't try to make people think you are something you are not. If people can't accept you as is, they are not worth it.

- Any person who judges you by your weight is an asshole. 'Nuff said.

- Sex is great (see more about sex in the next chapter), but don't give it away!

- Fat chicks can sometimes get desperate when looking for relationships. So please don't expect to find a steady boyfriend/girlfriend at the following places: Pool halls, dance clubs, mafia meetings, and bus stations at 3 a.m. In other words, if you are looking for a steady boyfriend or girlfriend, go to a place where you might find the most appropriate match. Don't get desperate and take whatever you can get.

- Always be friendly, but don't be embarrassed to state your opinions.

- Socialize with everyone. Don't be afraid they won't accept you. If they don't, move on to the next group.

- Don't do anything that makes you uncomfortable, but don't hide away from everything. It's time to stop being a wallflower. Socialization itself can be uncomfortable and awkward. Ease into it gently.

- Have a sense of humor. Learn the difference between humorous, not malicious jabs and outright fat hatred.

- Aren't getting invited to parties? Have your own.

- Flirt to your heart's content. If the object of your desire ignores you, he or she's an idiot, so move on to another.

Wow, I met this great guy/girl! What's next?

OK, you've met the right person. Now you need to keep the relationship going without listening to the inner voice that tells you that you don't deserve them. (Shut up, can't you see I'm writing a book!) Fat chicks can and do have good relationships. Don't listen to other people who say that you are "settling." You know inside whether you are or aren't, and if you know you are, get out — it is better to be alone than in a bad relationship! The only settling a fat woman should do is not to use looks as a standard. (We don't like it when people do it to us, do we?) Don't judge other people the way they might judge you. For example, my husband is very attractive but not in that Hollywood kind of way. Because of this, I was often told I was settling. But we have been happily married for four years now, and I know I never settled. (I once dated a guy who was conventionally handsome, and he turned out to be an asshole.)

Once you are in a relationship, remember that it should be based upon the foundations of love, trust, communication and a healthy sex life.

LOVE — You have to really love this person and love should be unconditional. Don't be with him or her because you think you can't get better. If you don't love your significant other you will be hurting them as well as yourself.

TRUST — You've been teased your whole life and there is always a possibility you'll get hurt again. Getting hurt is a part of life AND it happens to thin people too. You have to trust the other person in order for the relationship to work.

COMMUNICATION — Communication means listening to what the other person wants while they listen to what you want. Remember, both you and your partner are not the center of the universe. When you are together, you share that center.

HEALTHY SEX LIFE — You don't have to do it every day, every minute, but you should be doing it enough to satisfy both your needs.

OTHER TIPS:
Never stay in a relationship where your mate doesn't do 50 percent of the work (house and otherwise). Never stay in a relationship with someone who hits or belittles you.

Social groups and events

These groups are for fat people to get together. Some groups are social meetings, and some are purely to hook up.

....

BBW/BHM/FA ORGANIZATION: *http://www.bbwfa.com*
Lists events by states. Also includes a listing of online groups.

NORTHEAST

....

• HEAVENLY BODIES: *http://www.superbbw.com*
Heavenly Bodies serves the BBW, BBM and FA community with weekend-long dance parties in Massachusetts. Events occur every two to three weeks.

....

• BABS: *http://members.aol.com/bbwpittsb*
Serves the Pittsburgh area, and seems to have parties once a month. You must join their Yahoo! group for updates, as the Web site is still stuck in 2002.

....

• PHILLY BASH: *http://phillybash.com*
Philly Bash holds an annual three-and-a-half day party in, you guessed it, Philadelphia. Every year the party has a theme.

TRI-STATE AREA OF NEW YORK, NEW JERSEY AND CONNECTICUT

....

• LARGE ENCOUNTERS: *http://www.large-encounters.com*
Holds dance parties geared to singles every Friday and Saturday in

New Jersey, New York City and Long Island. Also offers online personal ads and an online newsletter.

- BABS: *http://members.aol.com/bbwwomen*
  Babs is a social club that serves the New Jersey area. Events are usually once a month and include pool parties, ski trips and theme parties.

- CLUB CURVZ: *http://www.clubcurvz.com*
  Serves western N.Y.

- GODDESSES: *http://www.goddessbbw.com*
  Goddesses offers dance parties every Saturday night, a yearly cruise, and a cable show. The dance parties are held around New York City. There is usually a cover.

THE SOUTH

- BBW SOUTHERN BELLES: *http://www.bbwbelles.com*
  BBW Southern Belles is an online service that runs social events for BBW women in Florida, Tennessee, Georgia and Louisiana. They also have a personals section. For general information, visit info@bbwbelles.com.

- BIG HOTLANTA BASH:
  http://www.bigbeautifulatlanta.com/hotlantabash
  Yearly party and conference in Atlanta. Costs for the 2004 Bash were $50 for advance tickets, $65 at the door.

- BBW OF FLORIDA:

  http://www.geocities.com/SouthBeach/Dunes/8511/links.html

  BBW of Florida is essentially a bulletin board of events in Florida. It also offers online chat and links for BBW adult sites.

- BBW FLORIDA CRUISE: *http://www.bbwcruise.com*

  For eight days and seven nights, enjoy this cruise from Tampa to the Caribbean and Mexico made exclusively for large-size people. Prices start at $480.

- GALORE: *http://www.clubgalore.com*

  This size-positive club is located in the Jacksonville, Fla., area. Parties are on Friday nights and often have a theme. You must be age 21 or over. Prices vary per party, though it is usually in the $5 to $10 range.

- KENTUCKY PLUS SIZE SINGLES:

  http://www.angelfire.com/ky/plussizesingles/index.html

  This singles club for Kentucky residents was started in 1987 and according to its Web site has been responsible for thirty marriages. The group meets monthly to plan activities like dinners, movies and other social outings. It also has had an annual hillbilly weekend. You can contact the group via e-mail at *pssclub@aol.com* or by phone at (502) 569-1838.

MIDWEST

- LINDA'S BIG CONNECTIONS: *http://www.lindasbigconnections.com*
  The largest plus-size gathering in the Midwest, they have dance parties
  in Chicago and Milwaukee. In Milwaukee, dances are held mostly
  once a month, once a week in Chicago. Besides dances, Linda also
  hosts hayrides, pool parties and other events.

- IN A BIG WAY: *http://www.inabigway.com*
  Serves the Minneapolis and St. Paul area with monthly events
  including dances, gaming nights and other events (such as picnics).
  Check out their message board for upcoming events.

- PEOPLE AT LARGE: *http://www.peopleatlarge.org*
  Hosts monthly social gatherings for BBW, BHM and their admirers
  in Minneapolis and St. Paul. You can join an e-mail list for updates.

- SAINT LOUIS BASH: *http://www.stlouisbash.com*
  Sponsored by Chub Club and Barb's Large and Lovely, a plus-size
  lingerie store (http://www.bll.com) Saint Louis Bash is a three-day
  annual party in St. Louis, Missouri. Contact Barb at *lingerield@ aol.com.*

- DANGEROUS CURVES AHEAD:
  http://www.geocities.com/daytonohiobbwparty
  Dangerous Curves Ahead holds dance parties every month in Dayton,
  Ohio. Contact them via e-mail at *daytonbbwparty@yahoo.com.*

THE WEST

- BBW OF AUSTIN: *http://bbwofaustin.moonvine.net/rings.htm*
  Contact them by e-mail at *bbwofaustin@moonvine.net*.

- BIG AS TEXAS: *http://www.members.tripod.com/bigastexas*
  Big as Texas is an annual size-positive event. It includes activist
  workshops, social meets, a fashion show and a keynote speaker.
  (Lynne Murray, author of the Josephine Fuller novels, was the
  keynote speaker in 2003.) E-mail *BigAsTexas@juno.com*.

- CLUB ENVY: *www.clubenvy.net*
  Serves the San Antonio BBW and BHM population with biweekly
  dance parties, many of which have themes. You can get in for free
  before 11 p.m. if you RSVP: *sherril@clubenvy.net*. Call (210) 568-8298
  for information.

WEST COAST

- BIG BOOGIE NIGHTS: *http://www.bigboogienights.com*
  This club, located in the very marvelous and lovely San Francisco and
  Fresno area, holds dances. Every event is in at a different location, so
  consult the Web site for directions.

- THE BUTTERFLY LOUNGE: *http://www.butterflylounge.com*
  719 W. 19th St., Costa Mesa, CA 92627. Located in the Lion's Den
  in Orange County, they offer dances from 9 to 2 every Saturday, as

well as special events, such as a New Year's party, and Karaoke on Wednesdays. You have to be 21 and over to get in.

• CLUB CURVES: *http://www.clubcurves.cc*
Club Curves offers two locations in California: San Diego and Redondo Beach. The Redondo Beach club (Pier 100 Fisherman's Wharf on the Redondo Beach Pier) offers dancing on Fridays and Saturdays with different themes. Friday's casual, Saturday is semi-formal. The San Diego club (6179 University Ave.) is open every Saturday night and is semi-casual (no caps, tennis shoes or shorts).

• NORTHWEST BBW: *http://www.bbwnorthwest.com*
Offers a listing of events, online groups, chat boards, personals and pictures for those living in the Seattle/Northwest area. Events occur once a month at different locations.

• VEGAS BASH: *http://www.bbwnetwork.com/vegas*
Yearly dance party that usually takes place in July. As of 2004, it costs $99 in advance, $129 at the door for the whole weekend (not including hotel). With the fee you get food, workshops, dance lessons and shopping.

ONLINE SOCIAL GROUPS

• BBW SINGLES: *http://bbwsingles.com*
A Web resource dedicated to big, beautiful women. The site includes chat rooms, articles, message boards and bios.

- SIRENS THE VOLUPTUOUS ENCOUNTER:
  http://www.bbwsirens.50g.com
  For large women and men. BBW's can post pictures and interests for
  people to e-mail you about.

Personals

I have listed only the sites that have a contact name, address and telephone
number or are a free service. When going on dates with strangers, always
meet at a restaurant or populated spot first. Double date if you can.

- BIG BEAUTIFUL WOMEN DATE FINDERS: *http://bbwdatefinder.com*
  Offers a free and a premium service. The free service allows your
  information to be looked at by other members and for them to
  contact you. The premium service allows you to contact any member.

- BIG DREAMS: HTTP://CELTICMOON.COM/BBW
  Big Dreams is a free service for BBW, BHA and FAs all over the world.
  You can browse by size, get people's e-mail and list your profile.

- PLUS SIZE PERSONALS AND BBW DATING NETWORK:
  http://plussizepersonals.com & *http://bbwdatingnetwork.com*
  Plus Size Personals and BBW Dating Network (both run by the same
  company) offer a free service in which you can receive and send
  e-mail from other members, search and browse their network and
  upload five photos. Although they are free, they require online
  registration where you need to give your e-mail and your stats. For
  the free service you can only contact the people who contact you first.

Premium service allows you to contact anyone in the network. Prices vary by how long you subscribe for (one month is $19.95; one year is $99.95).

- LARGE AND LOVELY CONNECTIONS: *http://www.largeandlovely.com*
Like Plus Size Personals, Large and Lovely Connections offers a free service where you can be contacted by any member of the network and a premium service where you can initiate contact. The premium service costs $29.95 for lifetime service. P.O. Box 421341, Kissimmee, FL 34742. (954) 489-2810.

- LARGE FRIENDS: *http://www.largefriends.com*
Large Friends is an online meeting area for plus-size singles. It costs $9.95 a month.

- LOVELY LARGE WOMEN: *http://www.lovelylargeladies.com*
Allows you a free ad with a profile and a picture. Membership where you can respond the to ads costs: One month for $14.95, six months for $34.95, eighteen months for $54.95 and thirty-six months for $79.95

Books

Arons, Katie. SEXY AT ANY SIZE: THE REAL WOMAN'S GUIDE TO DATING AND ROMANCE

"Sex is one of the nine reasons for reincarnation. The other eight are unimportant."

HENRY MILLER

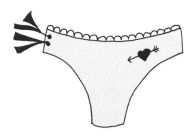

CHAPTER 15

SEX:
Fat Chicks Gettin' It Good!

There is a myth perpetrated by the media that fat women don't enjoy sex. Well, take it from me — it's a lie! I have sex on a regular basis, and I like it! And, I think many of my fellow fat chicks feel the same. A recent study in *Weight Watchers Magazine* revealed that 85 percent of fat women "always or usually" enjoy sex and that 70 percent almost always have an orgasm. This was compared with the *Sex In America* study, which found that only 40 to 45 percent of women reported regular sexual satisfaction and only 29 percent always had an orgasm. In addition, the *Weight Watchers* survey reported that 38 percent of fat women said they made love at least three times a week, 18 percent at least three to six times per week, and 2 percent every day, which is higher than the rates for thin women. Fat chicks are gettin' it, and we're likin' it, too!

Why do fat chicks enjoy sex more than their thin counterparts? One theory was advanced by Nobel prize-winning scientist James Watson, who co-discovered DNA. Watson believed that fat women are more sexual because their bloodstreams contain higher levels of leptin than thin people's. "Fat boosts production of endorphins, the natural mood-enhancing chemicals," he said. "And leptin, a chemical made in fatty tissue, helps create sexual desire." As I discussed earlier, leptin triggers production of the active form of a peptide in the hypothalamus, the small area in the base of the brain that controls hunger and metabolism. In other words, the same thing that makes us fat helps us to enjoy sex. A fair tradeoff, if you ask me.

My Sextory

Growing up, to me sex was something you saw in movies, read in books. It was something thin girls did with their thin boyfriends. In other words, it was something that I didn't do. It wasn't from lack of opportunity — there were plenty of guys who would bag me, if I had wanted to. While I didn't attract as many men as my thin friends, there were plenty of men out there who liked chubby chicks. My problem was that I bought into the belief that fat women were supposed to be asexual. I was so incredibly shy after being teased about my weight that I disconnected from my body as a something that could give me pleasure — my body was something to be ignored, not embraced.

My mind, on the other hand, was far from asexual. I thought about sex a lot and loved looking at porn. And, while I was open to other people's sexuality, the standards I had for others I didn't keep for myself. I shunned men throughout high school and college because I didn't feel I was ready for sex since I wasn't thin. I was afraid a man would reject me because of my fat body. I know that this was, and is, the experience for many of you as well.

Luckily, as I was on the road to healthy self-esteem and fat acceptance, I met a loving, patient man who I not only enjoy sex with, but enjoy marriage with as well. However, on some level, I still feel I am holding back from the pleasure I deserve, because somehow deep in my head I still feel that as a fat woman, I don't deserve to have sex. I am working to get past this, both on my own and with the help and support of my husband, but I think it is important for others to know that just because I have written a book called *Fat Chicks Rule!*, I still don't have all the answers, and I am still in many ways fighting the years of shame and rejection.

Sexual positions for large people

Enough with the bad feelings! It's time for the juicy stuff — how to do it as a fat chick! Before I start, let me tell you that many of the ideas in this section come from a wonderful site, *http://www.sexuality.org.*

BEFORE SEX: STRETCHING

In order to avoid cramping — or worse — try to stretch a little before you start. Remember, sex is strenuous exercise and uses muscles that you don't use walking down the street. Use the stretch as foreplay — or use your imagination.

THE MISSIONARY POSITION

...Or as George Carlin calls it, the "good old American man-on-top-get-it-over-with-quick." Place your behind on a stack of pillows or cushions, which will lift you high enough so that your partner can kneel between your legs. If you have a big tummy, lift it away with both hands, until the man gets himself positioned between your thighs. He can then insert his penis into your vagina fairly easily while holding on to you by your hips.

The only drawback with this position concerns women with extremely heavy thighs. However, if the man isn't too large himself (no pun intended) he can work himself between your thighs.

A variation on the missionary starts out with him between your legs, and inserting. Then you can lay your legs flat as he swings one leg over so that it's around your waist. Then you bring that leg toward the other one, and he swings his other leg over so that he's now straddling you. This requires a bit of practice, but once you perfect it, you can get some good penetration.

....

BACK TO FRONT, OR REVERSE COWGIRL
Sit on top, face your lover's feet, and insert his penis into your vagina from the rear. The only problem with this is that you may have to stay in a crouching posture while your man adjusts himself into a good angle of penetration. What you should do in that case is push his belly up before you sit completely, so he can rest it up against your behind.

....

REAR ENTRY, OR DOGGIE STYLE
Kneel on the bed with your legs slightly apart, then lower your chest so that your behind is elevated. Your man can then kneel behind you, and insert his penis from the rear. He can also rest his abdomen on your butt cheeks to make it easier for him to continue thrusting.

Rear entry can be a problem, especially if the man's penis is particularly short. To be honest, it is not my favorite position, because of the pressure it puts on my knees.

SIMS POSITION

A good position for when you are having sex with a thin man. Lie on one side, and draw your upper leg all the way up toward your head, so that the knee of the upper leg is opposite the hip of your lower leg. This makes your vagina easily accessible from above and behind. Your man then kneels behind you, with one knee on each side of her your straight leg, and enters from the rear at a slightly sideward angle. If necessary, he can raise his body a bit by means of a pillow below each knee.

UPSIDE DOWN POSITION

Lying on your side, turn yourself around so that your lover's head is at your feet, and vice versa. Then shift slowly until your genitals are aligned.

T-SQUARE POSITION

As you lie on your back with legs spread wide apart, your lover lies with his hips under the arch formed by your raised legs.

X POSITION

A modified T-square. Lie on your back with your legs bent at the hips and thighs spread as wide as possible. After his penis is inserted into your vagina, brings both legs together, while your lover swings his body 45 degrees (or as close as you can estimate while in the act) in either direction, forming a large X. Be sure to contract the muscles of your vagina to keep the penis from falling out.

········

STAND AND DELIVER

He lies face up over the edge of the bed with his legs together and his feet touching the floor. You then stand astride him, close to the edge of the bed. You can figure out the rest.

········

ORAL SEX

If you've been doing your stretching exercises, you'll be fine. Positioning is not generally a problem in oral sex, though if you are on top — or if you are lesbians and you take turns — be mindful of not hurting your lover below.

Books

········

Blank, Hanne. BIG BIG LOVE: A SOURCEBOOK ON SEX FOR PEOPLE OF SIZE AND THOSE WHO LOVE THEM

········

Blank, Hanne. ZAFTIG: WELL ROUNDED EROTICA

Fat admirers

FAT ADMIRERS (FAS) get off on the thrill of being surrounded and engulfed by fat partners. FAs are often viewed as fetishists by the non-fat mainstream, but they reject such labels as unfair, regarding popular culture as being dominated by a pro-thin bias. NAAFA supports FAs, believing "that a preference for a fat partner is as valid as any other preference based on physical characteristics, such as a particular height, eye color, or hair color." Since my husband is an FA, I obviously have no problem with this practice — after years of ridicule, I am tickled pink to be worshipped for my size.

FAs shouldn't be confused with feeders, who provide another person (the feedee) with an abundant supply of food to encourage weight gain, or simply delight in the act of feeding. Feeding is discouraged by the fat acceptance community.

"Thank you for being fat,
because if you weren't,
I wouldn't have the
rich life I do today."

CHERI ERDMAN, NOTHING TO LOSE

ENDNOTE

Size-acceptance links

BBW/BHM/FA ORGANIZATION:
http://www.bbwfa.com

BGN BIG GIRLS NETWORK:
http://www.bbwconnex.com/classifieds/main.php

BIG BEAUTIFUL BRIDES:
http://www.bigbeautifulbrides.com

THE BODY POSITIVE:
http://www.thebodypositive.org

BUNKIE LYNN:
http://www.bunkielynn.com

CAMRYN MANHEIM ONLINE:
http://www.camryn.com

CASS ELLIOT:
http://www.CassElliot.com

CLUB BBW:
http://hometown.aol.com/clubbbw/information.html

CURVACEOUS MAGAZINE:
http://www.curvaceousmagazine.com

DEBORAH VOIGT:
http://www.deborahvoigt.com

EMME, SUPER MODEL:
http://www.emmesupermodel.com

FAT ACCEPTANCE STUFF:
http://www.casagordita.com/fatacc.htm

FAT AND TERRIFIC:
http://www.infoasis.com/~avery/fat.html

FAT! SO?:
http://www.fatso.com

GRANDSTYLE:
http://www.grandstyle.com

I'M A BIG GAL:
http://www.imabiggal.com

JACKIE GUERRA:
http://www.jackieguerra.com

JANNY GIRLS:
http://www.jannygirls.com

JOYCE ANN MUDD — THE ORIGINAL MUDD WOMAN:
http://www.muddwomen.com

KATHY NAJIMY:
http://www.kathynajimy.com

LARGE DIRECTORY:
http://www.largedirectory.com

LARGELY POSITIVE:

http://www.largelypositive.com

MARGARET CHO ONLINE:

http://www.margaretcho.com

NO TO SOUTHWEST:

http://www.zaftig-2000.com/sandie/southwest.html

NOMY LAMM:

http://www.nomylamm.com

OBESITY SURGERY INFORMATION CENTER:

http://www.obesitysurgery-info.com

PLUS SIZE YELLOW PAGES:

http://www.plussizeyellowpages.com

SEXY EBONY:

http://www.sexyebonybbws.com

SHELLEY BOVEY:

http://www.shelleybovey.com

SIZE NET:

http://www.sizenet.com

SIZEWISE:

http://www.sizewise.com

VOLUPTUOUS WOMAN COMPANY:

http://www.volupwoman.com

Blogs

BIG FAT BLOG: *http://www.bigfatblog.com*
The best blog for fat news. This regularly updated blog discusses current news, articles and issues for the large-size person.

LIVEJOURNAL COMMUNITY: FAT GIRLS, NO CENSORSHIP
(Must be a member of LiveJournal to post but not to read):
http://www.livejournal.com/userinfo.bml?user=fatgirls
Fat Girls is a safe place for fat girls and their admirers. Discussion of weight loss is not allowed. Most of the posts are personal stories from fat girls around the world.

LIVEJOURNAL: CHUBBY CHICKS (Moderated, must be a member of LiveJournal):
http://www.livejournal.com/userinfo.bml?user=chubbychicks
Chubby Chicks offers a safe space to learn how to be size-positive. Diet talk is not allowed.

THE PRETTY PEAR: *http://www.prettypear.com*
Lots of women of different sizes talking almost exclusively about clothes. Some topics discussed include finding plus-size Halloween outfits, sleepwear and hot new clothes.

Heroes and Villains

HEROES

....

ELIZABETH FISHER: *http://www.ifisher.com*

This big, beautiful woman is petitioning Honda to include seat belt extenders in their cars. Please write her and say you support her cause, and also write Honda and tell them you won't buy one of their cars until they all have seat beat extenders.

....

CRYSTAL RENN

Lost sixty-five pounds in pursuit of her modeling career, then gained it all back and became a successful plus-size model

....

JURRIAAN KLINK AND JULIO RINCO, FREEDOM PARADISE

Jurriaan and Julio spent $2 million refurbishing two hotels in Mexico that are strictly for the large-sized.

....

THE BODY SHOP: *http://www.thebodyshop.com*

In 1997, The Body Shop created a doll named Rudy who was much larger than other commercial dolls. The accompanying ad campaign said, "There are three billion women in the world who don't look like supermodels and only eight who do."

PEOPLE MAGAZINE

For not once but twice picking plus-size model Emme as one of their most beautiful people.

NATIONAL ORGANIZATION OF WOMEN

For creating "Love Your Body Day" to call attention to disparaging images of women in ads and the media, as well as to enhance female self-esteem. It takes place every year on October 15.

VILLAINS

CLOTHING DESIGNERS FOR THE ANOREXIC

Versace, Guess, Diesel, Calvin Klein

PETA (PEOPLE FOR ETHICAL TREATMENT OF ANIMALS)

PETA has targeted fat people in their ad campaigns, such as one that said, "Don't Buy Two Seats, Go Vegetarian," implying that vegetarians can't be fat. Ingrid Newkirk, the president of PETA, once said, "We're not fighting fat people, but we are fighting fat. Used to be you would look around and there might be one fat person, and now you look around and the floor is shaking."

....

HONDA

Refuses to offer seatbelt extenders.

....

UNION PACIFIC

An example of a company trying to do the right thing for the wrong reason, Union Pacific instigated a wellness program that resulted in lower cholesterol, lower stress and less smoking for their employees. However, since the employees are still fat, Union Pacific is now prescribing diet drugsand dieting manuals.

"We're not giving up, and we're not letting ourselves go. Rather, we're forging a new relationship with our bodies, one that doesn't involve self-loathing, one that appreciates the miraculous bodies we have, one that brings joy."

MARY RAY WORLEY

THE FUTURE
FOR FAT CHICKS

lthough the world still has a long way to go on its road to fat
acceptance, I am optimistic about the future. Through the
activism of writers like Laura Fraser, Paul Campos, Jennifer
Weiner and Marilyn Wann, the actions of organizations like NAAFA, and
the growing awareness that fat is not as bad as it was cracked up to be,
things are looking positive for the future.

The marketplace is beginning to recognize the buying power of plus-
size women. The book you hold in your hands is just one of the many
size-acceptance books that are filling the market. Stores such as Old Navy,
Ashley Stewart and Lane Bryant are starting to recognize that they need
to offer big sizes. Torrid is one of the fastest growing clothing chains in
the country. Even the Gap and Banana Republic are considering carrying
plus sizes.

In the medical community, the debate is heating up on the "fat
and fit" argument. A *Consumer Reports on Health* (available on the *Consumer
Reports* Web site) article sums it up by saying that "recent studies indicate

that regular exercise and a sound diet may significantly offset the risks associated with excess fat." The article goes on to say that "some researchers have even suggested that inactivity — not obesity — is the true risk factor for premature death." A 2003 *Washington Times* article stated that more hospitals and doctors are buying equipment designed exclusively to treat fat people.

Things are improving in the workplace as well. A 2003 study called "America at Work," done by the Employment Law Alliance, found that 47 percent of workers believe obese workers suffer discrimination, 32 percent think obese workers are less respected, 31 percent say there should be government protection of the overweight, and 30 percent believe that obese workers are less likely to be hired or promoted. This indicates that the mainstream is beginning to accept that there is something wrong in the workplace, and that something needs to be done about it.

Media attitudes are also starting to acknowledge the changing attitudes toward body size. The February 2003 issue of *Teen Vogue* had as its cover headline: "Making It Big: How Curvy Girls are Changing Hollywood's Stick-thin Standards." The issue featured, among others, the story of Marissa Jaret Winokur. Atoosa Rubenstein, the editor of *Cosmo Girl*, says that her readers are "less obsessed" with attaining the model-thin ideal. "My generation was self-hating — we really thought we had to look like supermodels." Andrea Marks, author of *Healthy Teens, Body and Soul* says that messages like these "are a backlash to years of other unhealthy messages."

So, it looks like the world is heading in the right direction. But the fight is far from over. We still need to have a world where all shapes and sizes are accepted, where women don't diet themselves to death, where fat is treated as something normal, not abnormal. My fellow fat chicks, we have come a long way, but we still have a long way to go. Like any movement, there are going to be setbacks and disappointments. But, based on what I have seen in my lifetime, we are well on our way to a future where fat chicks rule!

About the author

LARA FRATER is a New York City-based fat acceptance activist who has struggled for years to find the perfect pair of jeans. But, after writing this book, she doesn't worry about that anymore. Her website is *www.larafrater.com*.